The Musician's Survival Kit

THE MUSICIAN'S SURVIVAL KIT
How to Get Work with Music

Leonard Pearcey

with a Foreword by Sir Peter Pears

Illustrations by ffolkes

BARRIE & JENKINS
COMMUNICA - EUROPA

To Selfridges

ISBN 0 214 20579 7

Typeset by Computacomp (UK) Ltd,
Fort William, Scotland and
printed by
The Anchor Press Ltd, and bound by
Wm Brendon & Son Ltd
both of Tiptree, Essex

Acknowledgements

My sincere thanks on the birth of this book, following its inception when I met my
editor at a Selfridges lunch, go to:

Sir Peter Pears for his Foreword and Michael ffolkes for his illustrations;
Lady Barbirolli, Anthony Burley, David Jacobs, Griselda Kentner, Louis Kentner,
Maureen Lehane and Yehudi Menuhin for their stories, and Ann Hughes for
David's;
Sir David Willcocks, Director of the Royal College of Music, and Robin Golding,
Registrar of the Royal Academy of Music, for their support and interest, and for
finding two students, Jonathan Rennert and Jane Highfield respectively, to act as
guinea pigs; and to Jonathan and Jane for being such appreciative guinea pigs;
Millicent Bowerman, now Literary Editor of the Gulbenkian Foundation in
London, for realising that the whole thing was her fault in the first place and thus
checking the book out for me;
Eunice Mistarz for being a marvellous secretary;
Peter Child and Bilbo Baggins for backing and patience during the gestation
period that must have seemed like nine months just the same;
and my editor for making it all possible.

Leonard Pearcey
Wimbledon 1979

Contents

Foreword
by Sir Peter Pears

If you are a young starry-eyed musician who has just received a distinction in Grade
VIII and thereupon decides to enter the profession, you may just possibly imagine
that all you have to do is to go on practising x hours (and more) a day, and you are
made. So Leonard Pearcey reminds us that this is unlikely – there are a great many
things to be done strictly outside music which are most probable (if not inevitable)
to 'make your career' and certain to help it. Much of the advice which this useful
book gives you may be thought to be fairly obvious, yet it is very easy to overlook.
And hardened old campaigners may well say to themselves 'I *wish* I had done that'
or 'I never thought of that'. This does not mean that if the young simply obey Mr
Pearcey's advice they will become stars and be able to buy their mothers a white
Cadillac. The book says practically nothing about music – that is not its prime
purpose. So by all means read this book and profit from it, but do not – repeat *do
not* – give up a moment of your x hours of practice, or any of your efforts to
understand and reveal the glories and magic of great music. That after all is the
point of it all.

Preface

What is now set before you in this publication with the title *The Musician's Survival Kit* has in its brief life been called by various other names: 'The Young Musician's Seminar', 'The Music Business – How to Get In and Get On', 'Making A Start: The Young Performer – How to Get a Booking and What to Do with It', and even 'Doh Ray Mee – or – Sol Fa, So Good'. Titles are always difficult things to choose, but really *The Musician's Survival Kit* sums it all up, and only a few words of explanation are necessary at this stage.

I'm assuming that you're a young musician at the start of a career, a career in which you only have either yourself as a soloist to think of or yourself plus an accompanist or yourself as the organiser for an ensemble you perform in. I'm also assuming that you're thinking in terms of getting work on the concert platform or the recital platform.

This means that I'm not really looking at careers in orchestras, opera companies and so on, which have a very basic procedure, and in which once you're in you tend to stay in. Nor am I looking at work outside this country. But at the same time the advice given will not be restricted to the recital platform or the concert platform, because in the early days you'll need to spread your wings very wide indeed in order to get as varied a range of experience and sources of income as you possibly can.

With luck, you're reading this before you leave the protection of a music college, but if not, fear not, because the advice still applies and it's never too late to start. From this I hope that established musicians will be encouraged to read what follows and also that as many teachers as possible, whether teaching privately or working within the confines of a music college, will continue to read it. Because over the years I've discovered that the advice that I'm about to impart to you is by no means general knowledge, and many well-established musicians and teachers have been quite surprised by some of the information: one very distinguished internationally known concert pianist, for example, didn't even know of the existence of telephone-answering machines.

If you're a conductor or a composer, then also please read on, because the advice given here can easily be adapted to suit your individual needs; in fact again, over the years, this advice has been adapted by jazz musicians and by ballet dancers, because the basic underlying principles are the same in many areas. And if you're someone in a position at any time to offer work to young musicians, then read the two-way traffic bit at the end of Chapter 1 and you'll see this is a book for you too.

The fact that you're reading this Preface would indicate that you've already looked at the table of contents, and possibly flipped through the pages and glanced at the headings of the various sections within the different chapters. If so, and if your mind is boggling slightly, let me boggle it even further by placing one or two caveats before you get into the work proper.

Much of what you read may seem very obvious to you, but experience has shown that each item will be new to somebody, even though this basic sort of advice is not new. To the best of my knowledge it's never been assembled in this way before, or in so much detail. In one or two instances I'll have to generalise, in others I'll have to be fairly exhaustive in order to be comprehensive, but by virtue of the changing nature of our world of music the book as a whole cannot be exhaustive nor is it a golden key. Clearly many of the examples will be personal ones because, as the first chapter explains, this is a book that is based on personal experience, and although I'm looking at the 'serious' musical field, you'll find reference to many other areas of employment.

But please don't think that you only have to read this book in order to get work. Besides your talent a fair amount of effort is going to be required on your part because on emerging from your music college, having been taught how to sing, or play the piano, or play the violin, or whatever skills you have acquired, the world is not going to come rushing to you. It's up to you to stand up and shout and let the musical world know that you now exist.

This introduction began with various titles for the advice that you're about to read; I suppose it can end with one more version: 'How to Stand Up and Shout and Tell the World That You Exist'.

It's up to you to stand up and shout
and let the musical world know that you now exist

I
Presenting the Pearcey Credentials

If the book in which you are reading this particular chapter actually belongs to you, having been paid for in good hard-earned or hard-granted cash over the shop counter, then presumably you have decided by now that I *am* the person to offer the advice that will help you to survive in the world of music. If, however, you are scanning this in a bookshop, then this is the chapter that I hope, apart from any brilliant notes on the flyleaf, will encourage you to take this little volume over to the counter and present your hard-earned hard-granted cash, because this is the chapter in which I explain to you why it is that *I* have written this book, and how the advice in it came to be collected together in its present form.

As I warned you, throughout the book inevitably there will be personal examples to illustrate the value of what I am telling you, so, equally inevitably, this particular chapter must include a little bit of Pearcey background, for those of you who have not encountered my voice in song or speech, or have not caught me on television, radio or discs, or in any other medium.

I was fortunate in attending a highly musical school, Christ's Hospital, so the fact that I sang a great deal came about almost by accident. I was equally fortunate in reading economics at Cambridge University, not just because the economics and the business training that went before it and the business experience that followed it gave me a very good basis for the reality of the world in which eventually I was to make my career, but also because at Cambridge I was a member of the famous *Footlights* revue team, and I ran a society which performed several charity concerts a term in widely different venues, from old people's homes to mental hospitals, from prisons to shows for the public at large. In performing in all these different kinds of shows and in performing real high-flown *Footlights* material, and in continuing all the singing that I'd learned at school, I was learning how to be a performer, how to cope with different audiences, different material, and different repertoires. So I didn't only learn by years of study, I also learned the way of experience, out in the sticks.

At the time too I was involved in what I later learned was called Administration in the Arts: a group of Cambridge friends (mostly King's choir men) and I had formed a singing group which became known as The Baccholian Singers, trail-blazers for The Scholars and The King's Singers, and during the long vacation we would tour in the West Country to raise money for charity, in fact for spastic children. I was responsible for organising those tours and I did what seemed to me to be the commonsense thing: I wrote to a large number of hotels and holiday camps and pubs in the area and asked if we might come to sing in order to raise money for this worthy cause. I also wrote to radio stations, to television stations, to the local press, and once again, while pursuing my normal studies and career, I learned how to organise a tour, how to get bookings, how to put programmes and brochures together, how to get publicity.

When I finished my university studies I went first into business, then into teaching, and on both occasions I was running the group and singing with them as a paid hobby, for they were now 'professional'. Eventually my career led me full-time into Administration in the Arts (including a spell as Company Manager for the New Opera Company), and when this happened I had to give up singing with the Baccholians, and concentrate instead on my solo career, again as a paid hobby, giving one-man shows, concerts, recitals, cabarets, just me and my guitar, and doing arts broadcasting and general broadcasting on radio and television. Initially while I was doing this I was working for Ian Hunter on festival organisation, handling tours for overseas orchestras, and managing the careers of international artists, getting *them* work, dealing with *their* brochures, *their* publicity photographs and so on.

Then I became Music Director of the Guildhall School of Music and Drama, arriving there with the qualities that the then Principal, Allen Percival, required, including a mixture of sound administrative training and experience, and a great deal of professional experience as a performer in virtually all the fields into which the young music or drama students might well go as a career.

In my very first week I was invited to a City livery-company dinner at which the entertainment was provided by a group of students from the Guildhall School of Music and Drama. Of their musical skills there was absolutely no doubt

13

whatsoever, but the way they walked on and off the little stage, the way they were dressed, the way they introduced the programme and the way in which that programme was put together, were not of the same standard, and the distinguished liveryman sitting next to me said, 'Is that the best you can teach your students, Mr Pearcey?'

The next day in the professors' club I raised this point with some of the professors, and they pointed out, quite rightly, that they had their time cut out in the limited hours available – in the limited years available – teaching their students how to sing and how to play, and there was in fact very little time to give them the hard, practical advice of the kind that I had seen to be needed. Very soon students, knowing that I was active in the profession, albeit in those days as a hobby, as a second career if you like, and that I was ready and willing to plug that advice gap, would come and ask me, 'Mr Pearcey, how do we get work in the music business, how do we find an agent, how do we put a brochure together, how do we approach people?'

Soon the handing out of this advice became another major part of my job as Music Director at the Guildhall School of Music and Drama. I found that some of the professors were not able to do it, either because to an extent they were out of touch, having retired from or only ever in a very limited way having been involved in the kind of activities on which the students needed guidance; or if they were younger and very active in the profession, conversely they were hardly ever in the school because they weren't able to devote that much time to teaching and in that limited time they had to teach the student to play trombone, or play percussion, or sing contralto, or whatever it might have been. And there was a similar problem at the other major colleges. Furthermore the students knew perfectly well that unless they landed an agent immediately they left school, they just would not get that kind of advice; and probably still wouldn't get it even if they were full-time on that agent's books and certainly not if they were on the books of a number of different agents.

All this caused me to take a much closer look at, among other things, début recitals and the way in which they were organised, and with one or two exceptions, I found that they seemed to work on the sausage-machine principle in that they gave the young person a platform without adequate preparation for that platform and without any kind of follow-up to the début recital. Consequently, when I left the Guildhall School of Music and Drama to concentrate on my own performing career I established, with the financial and moral support of Guinness (especially their Chief Information Officer Michael Hadfield) and Wedgwood (especially their Press Officer Judith Turner), a series of début recitals at the Purcell Room in which not only did I provide the students with a platform and an audience containing all the kind of people that ought to hear them, but also I gave them the kind of planning advice that is in this book, the kind of advice that I had learned myself after a great deal of hard work from experience on 'both sides of the fence', and the kind of follow-up advice that was necessary.

Then the Fairy Godmother appeared on the scene in the person of one Millicent Bowerman, who at that time was Deputy Director of the Greater London Arts Association. As many young musicians are well aware, the Greater London Arts Association organises a Young Musicians Scheme designed to give young people opportunities, platforms in the music business. Millicent felt that the kind of advice that I was passing on informally to the young people in my own scheme, the kind of advice that I had passed on informally to students at the Guildhall School of Music and Drama, should be presented to the Greater London Arts Association Young Musicians in a formal seminar.

Now those of you who *do* know me as someone who is very willing to perform on stage or screen or radio at the drop of a contract will be surprised to learn that in this particular instance I was backward in coming forward. But Millicent cajoled, persuaded, encouraged, and so, a few years ago now, I gave the first of my seminars for the Greater London Arts Association Young Musicians. I gathered together formally the advice that I had given informally, I mapped out a set of lecture notes and, with a certain amount of diffidence, uttered the first words of the first of those seminars. And even I who knew the tremendous need for this kind of information was amazed at the copious note-taking that went on, and amazed but also obviously gratified at the tremendous thanks that were given at the end of the seminar.

Now as a cross-check to my own information I had suggested that at that first seminar a number of distinguished people from a great many different areas of the world of music should be present, invited to comment on what I had to say as well as make their own direct contribution to the seminar. Something else that was gratifying was the tremendous response from the people who were invited, and I made notes of their comments on and confirmation of what I had to say and their own original contributions, and that was a pattern that has been adopted at every seminar that I have given since, not only for the Greater London Arts Association but also for the Royal College of Music, the Royal Academy of Music, the London

Opera Centre, the Incorporated Society of Musicians – on each occasion there have been, even if only two or three, experts from different areas in the musical profession who have commented on and contributed to what I had to say.

To detail the many names and positions would be confusing, as a number of them have since changed jobs or retired or gone abroad, but these included leading performers, agents, festival directors, orchestral managers, senior members of the Arts Council of Great Britain music staff, recording-company managers, music-club organisers, music journalists, representatives of the National Federation of Music Societies, the Head of Music Programmes from B.B.C. Radio, young musicians, college representatives, and students of all kinds, some of them now themselves established musicians who have come in their turn to contribute to seminars for their successors.

Let's end this particular chapter with two thoughts: first of all, while this book is designed to help the young musician, the embryonic performer, the person about to launch into a career in music, it is also very much about two-way traffic: it is also to help the music-club organiser, the television producer, anybody in a position to book young musicians. Young musicians can help them, they can help young musicians. This isn't just an exercise in selfishness. For example, the chapter addressed to the young musician and headed, 'Helping Those Who Book You' is very clear evidence of my determination to make this two-way traffic.

But also I hope very much that in reading this publication, potential bookers of all kinds will become aware of some of the problems of young musicians, just as many of the experts who attended my seminars from different areas of the musical world went away aware of difficulties for the young musician that they the experts hadn't even known existed. By making 'both sides' more aware everything can only be better all around.

And I like to think that one of the things that helps me to give such broadly based advice in this book is that I have always sat on 'both sides' of the fence. Not only have I been an artist in search of work, but also I've been, from the time I was with Ian Hunter through my work at the Guildhall School of Music and Drama and latterly after five years as Director of the Merton Festival, a person to whom other artists have come seeking work.

The second thought is, if you like, a put-down for the whole of this approach, because it's a quotation from a letter received from one of the distinguished experts who attended the very first seminar, namely Anthony Burley, the General Manager of the Eastern Authorities Orchestral Association. And in accepting the invitation to the seminar on 25 January 1973 he wrote:

I shall be delighted to attend but, dearly as I love giving advice, I shall be somewhat at a loss on this occasion except to say:
a. Get a good agent;
b. Get some good photographs;
c. Make sure that biographical material is sparkling, and that it is kept up to date.
Apropos b, it is perfectly acceptable, indeed often highly desirable, for ladies to use for ever photographs taken when they were twenty. Men on the other hand should occasionally get some new ones taken, preferably by Karsh of Ottawa who has the knack of making the most senile dotard look like Socrates; very valuable.

I don't feel I can even charge expenses for those artificial pearls.
With best wishes.
Yours sincerely,
Tony.

Well, in fact, that's a very good summary indeed, but do, please, read on.

2
Presenting the Plan of Campaign

A glance at the contents page will give you a pretty good idea of what the book is all about but it's important now to put some meat on the bones of that particular skeleton. This is one of those books that you ought to read right the way through before actually following the plan of campaign to get an engagement. But if you are a dipper or a browser, if you are an established musician or a teacher merely needing help on certain specific points, then turn to the contents page and you'll be directed to the answer to the questions that you want to raise.

Turning now to the plan of campaign, let's imagine you, sitting at home, wondering just how you're going to let the music world know that you exist, are talented and are available for bookings. First of all, you need to surround yourself with certain basic material. This is covered in Chapters 3 and 4. By sending this basic material to people you make them aware of your existence, so the first step is to tell you what to send.

The second step is where to send it and that is in Chapter 5, an outline list of potential bookers, a list that is very extensive. If it is properly covered it would be surprising if it didn't bring you in at least one booking to make the whole of the effort and the exercise worth while. Having told you what to send and where to send it, clearly the actual method and timing of the approaches are essential, and this is Chapter 6, the how and the when of the sending.

Following Chapter 6 there is, as it were, an imaginary interval during which you get this one booking that makes the whole exercise worth while. This is Chapter 7. And from then on it is a question of dealing with that one booking and capitalising on it.

As has already been said, this book is very much about two-way traffic, and

Chapter 8, 'Helping Those Who Book You', is really all about how to return the compliment of somebody actually wanting to employ you for your musical talents, and making sure that they don't regret their decision. Chapter 9 is all about helping yourself, because your musical talent and abilities alone are not enough to ensure that the particular booking is carried out properly. There are many other things to be thought of, and once you have read what they are you will find that they are very much common sense, but like so many other things under the heading of common sense, it helps to have them pointed out to you in the first place.

We then turn (Chapter 10) to the development of the one booking that you have obtained, how without necessarily going through the whole exercise in the first part of the book all over again you can build on that one booking. And then in Chapter 11 we discuss building on the investment that you made by undertaking the processes recommended in this publication. You will have invested a certain amount of money, but not a great deal in total in relation to the return you can expect to get on it, and you also will have invested quite a lot of your time. It will be a very worthwhile investment that will continue to bring returns in future years, but it is one that you will want to build on and develop as far as possible. One such development is the début recital (Chapter 12).

In Chapter 13 I take everything one stage further, both in a forward and a slightly backward sense, to give you some ideas on the development of your career beyond the areas that will have been outlined in Chapter 5, the where-the-work-comes-from chapter, and also an outline of some fall-back security avenues, as well as a little section on the icing on the cake, that is, the kind of booking that might not actually be directly in the line of career that you wish to follow but the kind that will certainly help you to live and exist while you are building your career in the chosen area.

Chapter 14 is probably the most serious chapter in the whole book, and is certainly an area that most musicians prefer to know nothing about at all, except for those rare animals who are organisers in their private life as well as being talented musicians; it is a very important chapter indeed, because it discusses the business side of your affairs. Chapter 15 is not necessarily a chapter like the preceding ones that tell you all the things that you have to do yourself in order to get work, but it does guide you as to the kind of people that you should surround yourself with and whose names should feature very prominently in your diary, who can make sure that the rest of your life, from a legal, health, monetary and security point of view, is well ordered so that you can concentrate exclusively on your musical abilities and your musical career.

And just as this little chapter and what has gone before have been setting you up for what lies in store in the main part of this book, the conclusion, Chapter 16, is designed to tie up any loose ends that may exist.

A reminder: at this stage I do want you very much to read the book in its entirety before you start following the plan of campaign, because by so doing, if you are a young musician at the start of your career, all the instructions and all the actions that you have to carry out will be seen in their proper context.

And this is where the story really starts.

3
The Tools for the Job or the Contents of the Kit I: For the Brochure

So you're sitting at home, ready to launch into the kind of mailing I'll be suggesting. What do you surround yourself with?

Photographs

Any photographs you have to send out as publicity material or to use in any way at all in connection with your future career must obviously be good photographs, by which I mean they must look like you, they must show where applicable what you actually play, they must reflect the kind of image or personality that you are trying to promote through your career. You should have more than one pose, and the photographs you use should be chosen by somebody else, because usually the pictures that you think make you look absolutely fantastic are in fact not the ones that really convey best to other people what you are all about and what you as a performer or as an individual actually look like.

Then the photographs must be suitable for reproduction in the press or in programmes or on record sleeves and so on. And certainly when it comes to the press and concert programmes, recital programmes, there's no point in having pictures that on a record sleeve might reproduce beautifully with a pair of hands and a face emerging from a great area of blackness, because very often, perhaps in a paper where they aren't able to have such a good reproduction as on a record sleeve, such a picture would be lost completely and would be absolutely useless. So the definition in the pictures, and they should be black-and-white pictures, must be very clear indeed.

Don't, if you're getting on in years, have pictures taken through the bottom of a football sock that are all misty and romantic and make you look younger than you actually are, because once again they will not be suitable for reproduction in the press. Apart from being misleading. And if you're going to reproduce photographs in the press or in programmes then you must have the copyright in the photographs. So before you go along to a photographer to have pictures taken, make absolutely sure that the pictures you're going to end up with, the prints that you choose from the proofs that he submits to you, will, in fact, have the copyright vested in you.

Not only will this mean that you can have pictures reproduced in newspapers without having to obtain permission from the photographer every single time, but also it will mean that you can take these prints to have reproductions made from them. Now reproductions are in fact copies of the photograph. What happens is that a photographer takes your print – and I would advise that the prints are 10 by 8 ins. – takes your print and photographs it. From that photograph he produces a negative, and from that negative he reproduces your print in bulk in the form of reproductions. These are to all intents and purposes just as good as the original prints and a great deal cheaper, and you can find someone to do it for you through Yellow Pages.

The choice of the original photographer is not necessarily a difficult problem and cost isn't necessarily the deciding factor. Expensive photographers need not be better than less expensive ones, but cheapness can sometimes be a very bad guide if the quality of the results is just as cheap. Very often you will be able to ask colleagues who are perhaps a year or so ahead of you in the development of their career where they had their pictures taken. Have a look at those pictures and see whether or not the kind of image that is promoted through them for your colleagues is the kind of approach from a photographer's point of view that you would want to see in your publicity photographs; or, perhaps, look at photographs of already established artists who may not be known to you or photographs in the press and find out by a letter or a telephone call who took them.

In this way you can select a photographer that you feel will be right for you. And if by any chance the photographs don't turn out exactly as you want them, but are good enough for use, then bear in mind another piece of advice, that you should have new photographs taken every single year. As was advised earlier in the book, don't continue to use for ever pictures that were taken when you were twenty; then when you have your picture taken again at the end of the first year, say, you'll be able to choose a different photographer, and during that year you will probably have discovered which particular photographer is right for you.

Having taken the trouble to get good photographs taken, photographs that tie in with all the advice given in this particular section, do keep a good stock of them available, so that whenever anybody rings up, whether it be an agent once you've got an agent or somebody who wants to book you or a newspaper which wants a photograph for publicity purposes, you always have photographs sitting there. If you don't have pictures available you're going to lose out on publicity opportunities. It never fails to surprise me that any number of established artists whom I have to contact in order to get photographs for publicity purposes – in connection with, say, a festival – reply, 'I'm very sorry – we don't have any photos available, nor does our agent.'

So the message here is a very clear one: once you've got the pictures taken, do keep a good stock of a set of different poses and *re-order* when that stock gets low, don't wait till it runs out. But don't over-order or you'll be tempted to use them up even when they're out of date.

Your Biography

For this you need to write round about 200 words, basically all about you from a musical point of view, and have it duplicated or printed. It should state where you were born, it should give details of your education and musical training (and if you're doing this on behalf of an ensemble rather than as a soloist yourself, then you should keep those details very brief indeed) and it should list all your achievements to date.

Don't immediately say if you're at the start of your career that you haven't really achieved anything, because by anything I don't mean Festival Hall appearances or tours of America (although obviously if you've done those, put them in). Even if you've only had one or two jobs under the protective wings of a college of music, then put those in, saying where you performed and what you performed. And of course if you happen to be the son or daughter of a famous musician and you're proud of the fact, or have any kind of famous relative at all, then pop that in, because a little bit of almost 'gossip column'-type information doesn't come amiss.

Just as you have to keep photographs up to date each year, so you must keep your biography up to date, because, all being well, as the result of the kind of exercise that's recommended in this book, you will get work during the first year, during the currency of a particular biography, so you'll have something to add to that biography in order to keep it absolutely bang up to date. If you keep a stock of the biography duplicated along with your stock of varied photographs, then you can

This is the sample brochure referred to on page 31 reduced here from A4 (297 × 210 mm) size to fit the layout of our book. Notice that everything has been arranged as recommended to fold into three and note also the accepted practice when using Press reviews to have three dots indicating deletions. Use this sample as a guide when discussing your own brochure with your printer.

TANIA ISLANDS was born in 1956 and educated in Oban. While a member of the National Youth Orchestra of Great Britain she became a pupil of Anna Queen, with whom she studied for three years at the Royal College of Music. After obtaining her Graduate, Performer's and Teacher's Diploma she won a Gerald Burley Young Musicians Award which enabled her to study with Clarrie Nette in Paris.

Since her return to this country Tania Islands has played in a number of our major orchestras including the Philharmonia, the Bournemouth Symphony and the Mozart Players. She has extensive experience of chamber music with the Scottish Woodwind Ensemble and other groups, and has given a number of recitals throughout the country. Her début at the Purcell Room in April 1978 received great critical acclaim. Solo appearances include one at St John's Smith Square with the Academy of St Martin in the Fields.

As a result of winning the BBC TV Young Musicians Prize she is to appear next season in a BBC2 recital, a series of concerts at Snape Maltings, four major festivals, and a late evening show at the Pitlochry Festival Theatre. Tania Islands is also well known in the dog world as a champion breeder of West Highland White Terriers, though her extensive recording commitments in the months ahead will curtail her showing activities somewhat.

CONCERTO

Busoni	Concertino, Op. 48
Copland	Concerto with string orchestra and harp
Finzi	Concerto with string orchestra
Hindemith	Concerto
Krommer	Concerto in E flat, Op. 36
Mozart	Concerto in A, K622
	Sinfonia Concertante, K297b
Nielsen	Concerto, Op. 57
Spohr	Concerto No. 1, Op. 26
Strauss	Duet-Concertino
Veale	Concerto
Weber	No. 1, Op. 73
	No. 2, Op. 74
	Concertino, Op. 26

RECITAL

Arnold	Sonatina
Bax	To The Wall
Benjamin	Le Tombeau de Ravel
Berg	Op. 5, Four Pieces
Brahms	Op. 120, No. 1 in F minor
	No. 2 in E flat
Debussy	Petite Pièce
	Première Rhapsodie
Ferguson	Four short pieces
Finzi	Five bagatelles
Hamilton	Three nocturnes, Op. 6
Hindemith	Sonata (1939)
Ireland	Fantasy-Sonata
Lutoslawski	Five dance preludes
Lutyens	Five short pieces, Op. 14, No. 1 (1945)
Martinu	Sonatina
Milhaud	Duo Concertant
Poulenc	Sonata
Rainier	Suite for Clarinet in A and Piano
Saint-Saëns	Op. 167 Sonata
Schmitt	Andantino, Op. 30, No. 1
Schumann	Phantasiestücke
Searle	Cat variations
	Suite
Seiber	Andantino Pastorale
Stravinsky	Three pieces for clarinet solo
Weber	Op. 47, Grand duo concertante
	Op. 33, Theme and variations

PRESS NOTICES

"Tania Islands bids fair to add her name to the lengthening list of significant English clarinet players . . . her confidence and technique are boundless . . . in Brahms's F minor Sonata, Miss Islands kept her tone compact, warm but not too vibrant throughout so that the eloquent slow movement sang sweetly without ever cloying. The third movement was appropriately graceful and the finale brimming over with high spirits." *The Times*

"Tania Islands is a clarinettist of high accomplishment. Her tone is smooth, yet pungent, and she played an ambitious programme with a remarkable degree of success at the Purcell Room.
In Brahms's Sonata in F minor, Op. 120, No. 1, she showed herself mistress of the broad phrase and rhetorical gesture . . ." *Daily Telegraph*

"A cut above the rest . . ." *The Lancet*

"The best Music Circle evening for many a long day." *West Sussex County Times*

RECENT ENGAGEMENTS
have included

South Bank Summer Music * Radio 3 'Young Soloists' Royal Dublin Society * Barrier Reef Coral Society Horsham Music Circle * Dyrham Park * ILEA Open University Club * Eton College * Hawnes School Wavendon Festival

FEE:

£100.00 including accompanist plus VAT and travelling/ overnight expenses where applicable.

All enquiries to:

MISS T. ISLANDS,
"Beckonmeback",
2, The Lakes,
Annua Lea.
RU2 N4T.
Tel: 01-359 3711

always type or write on a little extra sentence if you've just landed a Festival Hall performance or an American tour, and you can add that at the bottom of the little printed or duplicated biography.

Should you put your age or your date of birth on the biography? I must confess that I've always included my age on any kind of biography when it was required, although it seems to be the traditional thing among the ladies not to include theirs while the gentlemen usually do (a glance at *Who's Who in Music* will prove this point). And, of course, you can be too young; but there's one little story I would tell you to assist you in making your own decision:

The late David Hughes, a very fine singer and a good friend, who amazingly made the transition from being top of the hit parade to being equally successful in opera and oratorio, told me that for quite some time he never bothered to conceal either his age or his date of birth, feeling that both were actually irrelevant to his development as an artist. But when he passed the forty barrier he did start to keep quiet about it, not because it worried him in any way, but because he discovered that certain people felt that a tenor over forty wasn't capable of singing Don José. Now David had disproved this by being an eminently successful Don José when over forty. But at the same time, discretion in this case was definitely the better part of valour.

And although it's entirely irrelevant to this publication, there's another lovely story that David used to tell about an incident when he was transferring from the world of pop to the world of rather more serious music. At this stage he was touring in *Goodnight Vienna*, which one week was playing, apparently, in Walthamstow. Wondering how the show would go, David went round to the stage-door-keeper who was an old friend from his pop days and asked him what success he thought the show would have. 'Well, put it this way, Mr Hughes,' said the old chap, 'I think *Goodnight Vienna* will be as successful in Walthamstow as Goodnight Walthamstow would be in Vienna.'

Press Cuttings

It's always useful to know exactly what has been printed about you, by whom, and where. The easiest way to try and make sure that you get a copy of every cutting that appears about you in a major national newspaper or national magazine or major provincial newspaper is by joining a press-cuttings agency. Like so many other sources of information or help, you'll find these listed in Yellow Pages.

Ask around your colleagues for recommendations as to which agencies seem to be the most efficient from a musical point of view. The agency that I belong to has varied in efficiency from time to time ever since I actually joined it. The other day, for example, instead of being sent a cutting about Leonard Pearcey I was sent a cutting about Shirley Bassey. And for a while I kept getting cuttings about a Leonard Pearcey with different spellings who was conducting Gilbert and Sullivan down in Kent. I'm delighted to say that he was doing extremely well and getting very good notices.

But if you join a press-cuttings agency, then in theory every single time your name appears in print in a major national or local publication, then that agency will pick it up and send you a copy of what has been written. Not only is this very useful from the point of view of seeing how your concerts have been reviewed, for sometimes organisers will forget to send you a copy even if you ask them very nicely and give them a stamped addressed envelope, but also because you get indications of how your concerts are being advertised in advance. In my own particular case, for example, on the occasions when I offer an evening of songs with guitar, sometimes it comes through that my concert is being advertised as an evening with Leonard Pearcey and his guitar, or even as a guitar recital, and clearly by getting a copy of a cutting in advance I'm able to jump on this right away and make sure that it is advertised properly locally so that people don't turn up expecting a John Williams-type evening.

Unfortunately, on one occasion, in spite of all my precautions, I wasn't able to stop the way I was being advertised, and even when I got there, having told the lady who was introducing me that I was about to give an evening of songs with guitar, she stood up and announced that I was giving a guitar recital. And then after two hours, with an interval, of songs with guitar, she stood up at the end and said how sorry she was that I hadn't given a guitar recital.

On another occasion I was most inaccurately advertised as a folk singer. Now, I certainly do include some folk songs but would never describe myself as a folk singer. But the reviewer from a West Country paper, very much a folk freak himself in appearance as well as interest, even after having heard my evening, and having been told that the ad had been wrong, instead of taking the organisers to task, took me apart instead as if it were my fault. And he was inaccurate too. So I wrote to his editor, who offered to print my letter but with the reviewer's comments underneath (a privilege I'd have claimed myself in his position). You've probably seen how this gives the paper the last word, so even though I was in the right I dropped it. More of this sort of problem anon.

Repertoire List

This should be a complete list of all the items in your repertoire that you can if necessary play, as it were, at the drop of a hat. It should not be a list of pieces that you can play mixed in with pieces that you intend to work up shortly, because if an organiser sees that you play a certain concerto according to your repertoire list, and he's just had someone go sick two days before being due to play that particular work, if he gets in touch with you and says, 'I see you play such and such a concerto', and you only have two days in which to get it up, well, that's not going to do you any good and it certainly isn't going to do the organiser any good if you give an ill-prepared performance. So only list works that are actually in your repertoire, and that you could play at a moment's notice.

But don't restrict the list to 'serious' works. Do include any pieces of 'lighter' music that you are able to play, because a concert organiser often will wish, perhaps to make a good sale at the door, to include a lighter piece of music; as in so many other areas that you'll see in this book, versatility definitely does pay.

As with photographs and biographical material, keep your repertoire list absolutely up to date. As soon as you have a new piece in your repertoire, which you should work constantly to keep original and varied, add it to your master list, so that when you reprint it each year with everything else, you have an accurate, up-to-date list, and if you send out the list duplicated during the year prior to reprinting, then write or type on the latest additions. You never know who might be looking for a work that you have just added to your repertoire. And don't forget to include 'standard' repertoire pieces; your list doesn't have to be rarified all the way through. It should be of standard pieces, slightly more unusual and not so often performed works, and some lighter pieces as well, even jazz, folk or pop.

And just before anyone writes to me to say that there's no such thing as 'serious' music or 'lighter' music, let me say that I entirely agree and go along with Yehudi Menuhin when he says, 'There's simply Music, and it's great or it's good or it's bad.'

Engagements List

Your next list should be a complete record of every engagement you have carried out since you began performing. It can even include engagements fulfilled before you went fully professional or while you were a student. You should list the date, who you performed for or where (i.e. Wimbledon Music Circle or Wigmore Hall), and what you performed. Not only will this be invaluable to you should you be

Do include any pieces of 'lighter' music
that you are able to play

invited back to a place later on, but with any inquiry you can check if you have been there before, and you will know to say, 'How nice of you to invite me back', and you will know not to play exactly the same programme unless they particularly ask for it (that's always a tricky one; have they asked you back because they want to hear some of those pieces that were so successful last time repeated or to hear another part of your repertoire or a mixture? Ask them, to be on the safe side).

But also this sort of list will be of use to prospective bookers to know the kind of clubs you have performed at in the past, and it should include every single engagement, small ones as well as major national engagements. O.K., if somebody wants to book you for the Festival Hall it helps for them to know that you've had large-scale experience, but also if, perhaps, a very small music club wants to book you, then similarly it's nice for them to know that you have also been to and are happy to go to smaller clubs and organisations.

A Brochure
Once you've assembled a collection of photographs, a biography, a selection of press cuttings, a repertoire list, and an engagements list, you are ready to have a brochure printed. So quickly on to Chapter 4.

4

The Tools for the Job or the Contents of the Kit

II: The Brochure and Beyond

A Brochure

This need not be an enormously expensive, glossy, full-colour job first time out. The kind of A4-paper-size brochure that we've illustrated here in this book (based on the first sent out by the fine young clarinettist David Campbell) is quite adequate for a young musician at the outset of a career. Indeed, it would be quite adequate as an in-between-main-brochures hand-out for an established musician, because it shows what the performer looks like, and tells the organisers or the potential bookers a little bit about the performer's life, the performer's repertoire, the kind of press comments that have been made about him, and the kind of places at which recitals and concerts have been given.

If you don't want an expensive brochure first time out, then take your photograph, your biography, your repertoire list, extracts from your press cuttings (local press as well as national, for clubs like to know you went down well for organisations of their ilk as well as for Albert Hall audiences), and a summary of recent engagements (just saying who or where, not when and what), along to a duplicating or copy shop or instant print (address in Yellow Pages) and they will usually be delighted at no extra charge to arrange the things for you and inexpensively either photocopy or print them.

With economy as the watchword, your printer will be able to advise you as to the least expensive durable envelopes to take A4 folded, so plan your brochure with that envelope in mind, such that when you fold the brochure it doesn't crease across the photo or address details. Obviously if you send actual photos or repros you need a full-sized reinforced envelope and a PLEASE DON'T BEND sticker. (This explains the number of upright postmen you see around. Even though mine gets

31

me out of bed more mornings than I care to remember, I thank him for not folding things and forcing them through the letter-box.)

Remember when you go along with press cuttings not to take the press cuttings in full, just extracts. If you have one long cutting in particular that you want to send, then you can have this photocopied separately, and send it off with your brochure when eventually you send the brochure out. But do make sure that you only include genuine extracts from press notices: if for example the critic has written, 'If only there had been some brilliant playing ...', then it is definitely not right to use an extract from that quote appearing in your brochure as 'Brilliant Playing'.

The vital element for your brochure is your name (yes, I *have* seen it left off), address and telephone number. If at the outset of your career you are liable to be moving on quite soon from digs or some other kind of temporary accommodation, then you can get little instant stickers produced very inexpensively, as per the adverts in the national press on Sundays, and as shown on our example brochure. If then, having had the brochure done, you decide to move on, say, a week afterwards, all you have to do is get some new stickers done very inexpensively and stick them over the old ones. But do, I beg you, include your address and telephone number. It has astonished me in the past the number of brochures that have landed on my desk from people wanting me to book them for one thing or another without having an address on them to which I can reply or a phone number which I can ring. And if you're organising for an ensemble and the others (praise be) are helping, only have *your* name, address and phone number. It gets confusing otherwise.

The final element that I always like to see on a brochure, but this is a slightly controversial one, is fee and expenses, including accompanist and VAT where applicable. This is a very debatable point, and it's one of the points that I would advise you to discuss with those of your friends who are in the profession or who are about to enter it, so that you can work out your own policy on this. From my point of view, if I receive a brochure I like to have an idea of the fee and expenses of that artist in front of me if only to save me ringing up and then finding out that they are too expensive for the particular concert or project that I had in mind. This is really the first time that I have mentioned the word fee in any definite context in relation to the advice that's being given to you in this book. Don't be alarmed, that all I'm saying is state a fee, and immediately start wondering what that fee ought to be: we come back to this whole question of the level at which you should start on the scale and the amount of negotiation you should undertake later in the book, as you can see from the list of contents.

One final plea on the question of your brochure: please make sure that the spelling is correct. I accept the fact that if you can't spell to save your life, it doesn't necessarily mean that you can't play the violin or sing absolutely brilliantly, but if a booker – and this is the first time that I've mentioned this too, but we'll keep coming back to it: bookers *are* human – if a booker receives a brochure in which Lieder is misspelt or the names of certain major composers are misspelt, then they're not likely to form a very good impression of the talents of the performer. And however unfair that may seem to you, it is, sadly, a fact. It's a fair assumption on the part of the potential booker that if the brochure has been sloppily prepared, then the performance will be sloppy as well. So if your spelling is atrocious, then get the whole brochure checked through by someone whose spelling is good before you actually have it duplicated or reprinted.

Later on in life by all means have a more expensive brochure printed, but here again there's an interesting psychological point: don't get too expensive and too lavish, because again the human booker may look and say 'Golly, if this artist can afford to have a brochure presented as luxuriously as this, then that fee that I'm staring at is bound to be inflated.' This takes us into the question of images again, and the kind of fair or unfair conclusions that people seem to draw. I remember arriving for a recital once in a friend's MGB as my own car was laid up at the time; and I heard some young audience members commenting as they went into the hall, 'He arrived in a sports car so he must be good.'

A bit like the horrified look that apparently came across the face of a Sadler's Wells official when after an opera performance David Hughes gave him a lift home in the vast American car that was a legacy from David's pop days. Evidently not the right image for an opera singer. What a funny thing this image business is.

Publicity Material

Every now and then it's quite likely that some newspaper or magazine will print some kind of little 'personality piece' about you: perhaps a little snippet in a Diary about how marvellous you are, or perhaps even a full-length interview about you. If this happens, then it is well worth while having it reproduced, photocopied when you're having your brochures photocopied or printed, or having your major press notices reproduced in full. Then from time to time, as well as your brochure, you can send off a little biographical note in the form of a personality write-up from a newspaper or a magazine. These are very useful as back-ups to your brochures on appropriate occasions, as are testimonials from well-known and popular established musicians, which again you should reproduce in full, preferably having the entire letter photographed, assuming that you have the writer's permission, of course.

And don't stint yourself on the number of copies you have done. This kind of multi-reproduction is very inexpensive, and once you've had the basic plate made, then it's in your interests to get as many copies as you can possibly afford without overstocking, as with photos. One word of warning however: make sure when you're sending out a letter with your brochure, or a complete photographed press cutting, that it isn't actually about ten years out of date. Even if you've had other write-ups since then, people are likely to assume that the reason you're not sending any up-to-date write-ups is because you haven't had any, and perhaps your standard has 'gorn orf' in recent months.

Notepaper

Even if you have your name, address and phone number on your brochure, then you should also have your name, address and phone number on your notepaper as well. But why, you cry, should I have my name on my notepaper when I intend to sign the letter anyway? Well, the trouble is that very often people forget to sign letters, and equally often people who do sign letters have signatures that are almost completely illegible. And as the recipient of your letter may separate the brochure from the notepaper and throw one or t'other away, it's important to have name, address and telephone number on each.

If by any chance you feel that you're not sufficiently permanent in one particular place to have printed notepaper done, then once again, buy some perfectly ordinary respectable unheaded notepaper and use the little stickers to give your name, address and phone number. Then, as with the brochure, when you move, all you have to do is overstick new stickers on top of the little sticker of the out-of-date address. And although it sounds expensive, I recommend having not plain continuation sheets but using the proper headed notepaper for every part of the letter. Once again, if by any chance it's page 2 that's got the interesting information on and actually quotes the fee, and page 1 happens to get lost and page 2 hasn't got your name and address on it because it's a plain continuation sheet, then the booker will be very frustrated and you will possibly have lost the chance of that particular engagement.

Book List

In the early days of giving this advice I used to list quite a number of publications that would be useful to the young musician seeking future employment, but frankly, since the appearance of the *British Music Yearbook*, this is the only book you really need to own, with the possible exception of the *Music Education Handbook*. I do very sincerely encourage you to buy a copy of the *British Music Yearbook*. If you genuinely feel that you can't afford it at this stage of your career on top of the other expenses that you're likely to incur in an exercise of this nature, then by all means borrow one or refer to one in the local library. But as one of its values for you is the lists that it contains, it is much easier to have a copy in your own home rather than having to copy down long lists from various sections of the *Yearbook* while seated at a table in your local library.

The *British Music Yearbook*, as it states on its own flyleaf, 'provides an annual look at music in Britain. It contains authoritative articles and discussions on current issues within the musical world and a *large, comprehensive directory of the music industry*' (my italics).

The next chapter of this publication will indicate just how comprehensive the *British Music Yearbook* is and I'd better declare what is now an interest right away, in that in the *Yearbook* the advice that is given in this book in great detail is summarised virtually in note form in an article contributed by me at the request of the editor, Arthur Jacobs, entitled, 'Making a Start: The Young Performer'. The *Yearbook* also contains some other very useful articles that touch on some of the areas dealt with here, but its real value to the young musician at the start of his or her career is the lists it contains, as will be fully explained in the next chapter.

Apart from owning the *British Music Yearbook* and possibly the *Music Education Handbook*, you can of course consult all other works of reference or interest at your local library. You should certainly read a 'quality' national daily and Sunday newspaper in order to keep yourself up to date with what is happening in the field that you have chosen for your career. By this I don't just mean reading write-ups of concerts and recitals, but I mean reading all the news about what is happening in the world of music in particular and the world of the arts generally; and on the diary pages you will find little snippets of information about, for example, the wing-commander down in Herefordshire who intends to turn a barn into a concert hall, and is looking for young artists to launch his new season, or as I once read, the new arts programme that hadn't got a presenter which I was able to make my own.

A cassette made on good but simple equipment
in the comfort and privacy of your own home

If you don't feel that you can afford to subscribe regularly to one of the many excellent music magazines, then again you can consult these at your local library, and you certainly should consult the *Radio Times* and *TV Times* each week to see again what is happening in the field of music on radio and television, remembering that music doesn't only happen in music programmes, that, for example, light-entertainment programmes very often require signature tunes to be written or guest artists to perform. All of these publications, whether you subscribe to them regularly or whether you beg, borrow or otherwise obtain them, or refer to them in your local library, will keep you absolutely bang up to date on what is happening in the world of music in its broadest sense.

When you join the Incorporated Society of Musicians or the Musicians' Union or Equity – and the advice on which of these to join is also given later in this book – then you'll be entitled to subscribe to or buy or obtain free various valuable publications from these different organisations, so you'll end up with a mini reference library, and after all, the secret of any good organiser (which you'll soon be in relation to your own career) is knowing where to look for the information that you need.

Cassette Recorder

As you will have gathered by now, the next chapter is the promised one on where to send all this material that you're now collecting and very often you will find it invaluable to include on special occasions, with your publicity material or your brochure, a cassette that gives an idea of your standard of performance. It could be a cassette made on good but simple equipment in the comfort and privacy of your own home, or it could be a recording made, with permission, of a concert given for a music club or similar organisation. Take the help and advice of friends and experts.

And that mention of permission echoes back to the question of photographs and the question of copyright. If you're going to send out cassettes (have more than one if possible, to offer choice) of any performance of yours, even if it's only for quiet domestic-publicity use, then you must make sure that copyright has been properly taken care of. While a lot of people certainly get away with sending out recordings of their performance without having had the necessary permission, it really is advisable to be on the right side of the law at all times, and it isn't very expensive to get a licence from the Mechanical Copyright Protection Society Ltd which enables you to record music that is copyrighted for this kind of purpose.

When you do send out a cassette, make absolutely sure that on the cassette you have your name and address and telephone number – once again use the little stickers – as well as the title of the work and the date and, if it is a non-private recording, a non-domestic recording, the occasion on which the recording was made. Usually it is better to offer the cassette to people rather than send it out first time round, then if they're really interested they will phone you or write to you and say, 'Yes, we'd like to hear the cassette'; and if you do send it off, make a careful note in your filing system, of which more shortly, on what date you sent the cassette and where you sent it, so that if it doesn't come back you're able to get in touch with the person you sent it to and ask for it.

And while we're dealing with recording of performances, there's an important point that should be made even though it's a little early in the book, since it belongs here. If anybody wants to record your performance, then not only should they have the necessary copyright clearance for the works you're performing but also they have to get your permission and if you happen to be soloist with a professional orchestra, of course, the Union representative will come into it as well. If you do grant permission for your performance to be recorded, then make absolutely sure that it's only going to be used for domestic or possible educational uses. There have been occasions when people have asked to record a performance for private use, and then issued what is basically a pirate record of your performance.

People should have the courtesy to ask your permission before a concert starts, and of course it's difficult to stop in mid song if suddenly you notice a microphone suspended from the ceiling or sticking out of someone's pocket. Difficult, but it has been done. At this stage I simply want you to be aware of the rights and wrongs of the situation.

Typewriter and Filing System

Later in the book we'll discuss in a little more detail the kind of basic 'office' system that you ought to be operating to keep on top of your correspondence, but at this stage, as we're about to come to the sending out of the publicity material and brochures that you've gathered round you, let me say that you should if possible buy, but if not beg, borrow or otherwise acquire: a typewriter. If your handwriting is particularly good, a typewriter is still an advantage, because you're going to have to write quite a few letters at this early stage of mailing and letting the world know that you exist.

It doesn't have to be an expensive electric machine, although quite frankly there are some super inexpensive electric machines on the market, and they do make typing that much easier for the non-professional typist, but it should be a basic functional machine. If the 'e' drops or the 'h' shoots up in the air a little bit, it doesn't really matter at this stage, as long as whatever you send out, whatever letters you send, whatever labels you address, are legible, and you'll be surprised, if you can't do a little bit of typing already, how quickly typing will come to you even on a gentle two-fingered basis.

And as far as a filing system is concerned, well, it needn't be elaborate at this particular stage, as long as you have some way of keeping a record of what correspondence you've sent out and to whom your brochures have been mailed at the start of your career; when it comes to discussing actual correspondence in relation to each particular engagement gained as a result of this exercise, then we'll talk about a filing system in greater detail. But for now it'll be sufficient to buy perhaps a simple little box file and keep in it a record of all the information that you've sent out and where you have sent it, together with the originals of the materials that you used for photocopying.

5

Where the Work Comes From: Starting

So there you are, sitting at home, now surrounded by all those photographs and brochures and notepaper and envelopes (as recommended in the previous two chapters), and you want to start addressing those envelopes, so whose names and addresses do you put on them? Well, this is where the *British Music Yearbook* that you've bought or borrowed or referred to and the *Music Education Handbook* likewise really come into play, because they contain all the addresses that you need to carry out this particular exercise.

Remember that we're not really considering employment as a member of an orchestra or employment as a member of an opera company or employment overseas. We're really looking at employment, in the United Kingdom, of a one-off nature: concert work, recital work, for you on your own, or with your accompanist, or with your ensemble. So here we go.

Agents

If the whole point of this exercise to you is that you haven't got an agent, which is why you're actually doing it in the first place, then it's well worth getting in touch with as many agents as you possibly can, because even if one of them doesn't accept you on an exclusive agreement whereby all your work goes through them, the chances are that a number will be happy to have you on their lists to offer when they feel an engagement is right for you. This means of course that they won't work for you as hard as they would if they had you exclusively and therefore were getting all your ten, fifteen or twenty percentages, but it does at least mean that your name will be going into another area, or maybe twice into the same area, and running water does wear away a stone. If a booker you've been trying for years responds to the first agency mailing, or vice versa, that's life, and neither you nor the new exclusive agent need be upset. But the answer to: 'If we book direct and save you commission presumably you'll charge less than your agent' is 'No'.

So which agents out of the long list do you write to? The answer is that you write to all of them, unless they have a particular specialisation that does not refer to you. For example, if you are a string quartet, there is no point in writing to an agent that only deals with opera singers. You may have heard that some agents are particularly good, and some other agents are particularly bad. Quite frankly this kind of information is best completely ignored. There are distinguished artists who will swear by one particular agency which other artists wouldn't touch with a barge-pole, and this applies to every agency that you will find listed. So, be as wide-ranging as you possibly can. And, as hinted above, be fair to your agent when you do get one. Agents tend to get more brickbats than bouquets but they do provide a valuable service for artists and bookers.

Festivals

Here I'm not referring to the competitive festival, I'm referring to the festival of the Edinburgh, Bath, Brighton ilk. You'll discover from the *British Music Yearbook* that there are so many festivals in this country of varying shapes and sizes that you could virtually perform at one every day of the year and still have some left over for the year ahead. And nearly every festival gets a grant of some kind or other from the Arts Council of Great Britain or from a Regional Arts Association or from business sponsorship, so every festival basically is in a position to afford to employ you, a young musician at the outset of your career when your fee is not as high as I hope it's going to end up.

Schools

Many public and private schools organise a series of concerts during term time for their students, particularly if they have a music club. The ones with music clubs you'll find listed in the *British Music Yearbook*. Think back to your own school days, remember the kind of concerts that took place, the kind of recitals that were given, and what you liked or disliked about them, and this will give you a guide as to how to approach the directors of music at public or private schools.

You should also contact music advisers, listed in the *Music Education Handbook*, who organise, if their budgets permit, concerts for state-maintained schools. Very often you can build up a very nice tour of three or four days working for one music adviser in a series of different kinds of schools in his area. Not long ago I spent a tiring but rewarding week touring schools for the mentally handicapped in Richmond.

Universities
Here again the *Music Education Handbook* will help you. Where the university has a music department, then you should send your material to the head of that department. But the fact that a university doesn't have a music department doesn't mean there isn't scope for employment there. If this is so, it is worth writing to the president of the Students' Union or the secretary of the Music Society.

The National Federation of Music Societies
Not every music club or society, amateur choir and orchestra, belongs to the National Federation of Music Societies, but the bulk of them do, and you will find the majority of these listed in the current *British Music Yearbook*. This is perhaps the largest area of potential employment for the young musician of all those that I am listing, and you probably came across some of the smaller music clubs or societies, or choral societies and orchestras, during your student days.

The scope for employment here is so big because very often, all being amateur organisations and not necessarily always having access to any kind of grant aid, many of these societies tend to include the younger artist in the hope that fees will be reasonable and therefore their budget will not be too stretched. Clearly there are opportunities for performing as soloists with the orchestras or the choral societies, and although we're not really going into the question of orchestral employment or chorus work, there's also a good chance that you might be able to get some employment 'stiffening' the orchestras or choral societies while some of your colleagues perform the solo works out front.

Municipal Entertainment Officers and Arts Officers
Not many young musicians have come across these ladies and gentlemen, whose task it is throughout the country to organise entertainment and arts activities for their local authority. They may have theatres or concert halls or libraries at their disposal, they may have lavish arts centres, they may simply have various halls used for a variety of purposes. But this is the area where the lighter side of your repertoire may well come into play. This is because they have responsibility for 'entertainment' as well as 'the arts'.

Regional Arts Associations

It's well worth your while making yourself known to the people who run the Regional Arts Associations, as not only do they exist in an advisory capacity, and if they get an inquiry for the kind of music that you offer are able to pass your details on, but also they organise planning conferences and issue bulletins. These bulletins are a valuable free source of publicity, and once again will bring your name to a much wider audience. As far as the planning meetings are concerned, you should try offering to provide the entertainment at one such meeting or conference. Clearly, if you are accepted, while other people's brochures or publicity material will be lying around, you will be there in person, to be heard by all the delegates from, say, local festivals or local music clubs attending the Regional Arts Association's Planning Conference.

Radio and Television

The B.B.C. has a very definite national auditioning system, so you should write and apply. Either you'll be invited to a studio to be heard by a panel, or someone will come to listen to you at a recital or at a concert. But here again, you should cast your net as wide as possible, and let every local radio and television station, B.B.C. and commercial, know about your existence. You can never tell what is actually in the pipeline. A producer may be planning a particular programme featuring the works of a composer in whom you specialise, and will be delighted to receive your brochure and know of your existence and specialisation in the works of that particular composer.

Alternatively, your brochure may find its way on to the desk of a magazine programme producer looking for an unusual musical item for a magazine programme, or looking for a new young performer to inject fresh blood into a programme. Remember, you never know what's in the pipeline, so it's always in your interest to advertise your existence as widely as possible in the areas of radio and television, especially as individual commercial companies can have very different policies and audiences even for a localised programme are considerable. The microphone and camera experience at a local station is a great help in preparing you for major network appearances or auditions, and those local stations will celebrate national success with you.

And remember that radio and television don't only employ musicians in their own right, as it were, to give their own performances. Very often there will be a guitarist or a singer in a play, and here if your brochure reveals that you've had a certain amount of acting experience as well, then you'll be on the right lines for that particular producer. Series have incidental music, stations have identification music; keep your eyes and ears open for all the possible areas of employment in radio and in television.

Recording Companies

Nearly every young musician dreams of having a record or two as early as possible in their career. One of the problems is that major recording companies are very reluctant to take the risk of taking an untried talent into the particular strains that are attached to working in a recording studio. While some of the smaller companies may well be prepared to take that risk, and while certainly some of the bigger companies again may look at you if you have a particular specialisation or offer one or two works in your repertoire that have not perhaps been recorded, it is a sad fact that unless you can find someone to sponsor your recording by paying part of the fairly heavy initial costs of making it, then you will certainly not, at least at the early stage of your musical career, find your way into a recording studio.

There is, however, another method that is an interesting possibility, and that is to offer to take a certain number of records yourself. Very often a smaller producer will be delighted to have this guarantee of a proportion of sales, and by letting you have the records at trade price not only will he be assured of covering certain basic costs, but you will have records to take round with you to sell at concerts and recitals, and according to the arrangements that you've come to with the organiser of those concerts and recitals, will be able to boost your income through those sales – though you must of course remember the tax aspect of this sort of transaction. Don't worry about this at this particular moment in the book; later on, when you get to Chapter 15, you will find out which of your various specialists will look after you in this area.

And although I try not to be too repetitive in this publication, except for those particular remarks that I want to drum into you very securely, it's worth repeating here the advice to keep your eye on the music press for this may well bring to your notice a new recording company, just set up, and these newer emergent companies may well be interested in the repertoire of the younger artist. So, send your brochures to as many recording companies as possible, because you never know at what stage in their future planning they may have cause to refer to your material.

Orchestras

You may be surprised to find this particular heading in view of what I said about not suggesting in this publication how to get work *in* orchestras, but if you think back to the section on amateur orchestras, it won't surprise you to know that many of the smaller and younger professional orchestras could well be very interested in learning about the solo repertoire of an emergent young artist. And, of course, work *with* orchestras as soloists may be just what you're looking for, so it's still worth mailing to managers or conductors of major orchestras, though without an agent that's a big jump, and letters of personal recommendation from established performers will be a help.

Opera Companies

Another surprise perhaps, but all I said under Orchestras applies here too, except that for orchestras read opera companies.

Churches and Cathedrals

The study of your local newspaper and the music advertisement pages of the national press will show you which religious venues seem particularly interested in promoting concerts by young artists. Very often, as you will have discovered in your student days, they will hope that you will appear for nothing. While with luck you have got beyond this stage, unless you're working for a charity (and there's a lot more to come on this question of fees), it could well be in your interest to arrange a concert in a particular area merely to let people in that area know of your existence. (This will be developed further in Chapter 10.) Churches and cathedrals, of course, also have employment to offer for organists (several of whom have adapted the advice in this book to great effect) and occasionally, for professional singers, a little more icing on the cake as far as early finances are concerned.

Be Wide-ranging

These words have cropped up already in this particular chapter, but they're worth emphasising before we move on to the next section of the book. At this stage there is very little point in being selective, unless you genuinely haven't the time or money for the full works. (But wait for the bit on bank managers.) It is much better to sow all the seeds you possibly can, because even though some will come to nothing others certainly will germinate. Do not be disappointed if there is not an immediate response to every single letter that you send out. The fact that someone does not reply to you does not necessarily mean that your letter, your publicity material and your brochure have gone into the waste-paper basket. It could be that they have been working well in advance and have planned two or three seasons ahead, but that they like the look of what you have to offer and therefore are keeping your brochure on one side, with a view to approaching you on some future occasion.

It's also not a good idea to be selective, opting for London versus the provinces. 'But I don't want to go miles out into the sticks – I only want the big prestige dates in London.' In the first place you'd be very lucky early on to get the big prestige dates in any major city, and in any event at the early stage of your career it is in your interest to take on as many bookings as possible, to become as widely known as possible. This way you not only build up a reputation, you build up a following, you build up a strong potential audience. Do not scorn the smaller music clubs: not only may they be able to pay as high a fee as a much bigger club, they also may be much more appreciative of what you have to offer as a young artist than a club that has a lot of money to offer and can afford perhaps a whole series of big names.

And remember that the big names are not necessarily better than you are. Also you never can tell when the music-club organiser from a small club may suddenly become the organiser of a major festival that's held in that particular area. Or there may be somebody in the audience for the small concert that you give in a little country town who organises concerts for stately homes or major hotel chains. Once when I was on holiday in Cornwall, I'd taken my guitar with me to do some practising, and the landlord of the local pub who knew me well, in fact from those student tour days, said, 'Leonard, bring your guitar along one night and give us some songs: we're trying to raise money for charity.' So I took my guitar along, sang a few, fairly merry, late-evening songs in each of the bars, and a collection was taken for charity. Everybody had a marvellous time, and when I got back home, I received a letter from a very distinguished gentleman who just happened to be on holiday down there as well and who was in the pub that night, and who'd liked what he heard. As a result of that I got a series of very enjoyable bookings.

A Very Special Warning
As you already know, all the lists that you require to carry out a mailing of the extensive kind suggested in this chapter are to be found mainly in the *British Music Yearbook* but also, for schools and universities, in the *Music Education Handbook*. It is

I received a letter from a very distinguished gentleman
who just happened to be on holiday down there as well
and who was in the pub that night

vital that you only use up-to-date editions of these publications. Don't go to a second-hand shop and get an old edition of the *British Music Yearbook* to save money. It will be a false economy at this stage in your career. Organisers, clubs, addresses of festivals, names of producers, change very quickly indeed. The whole point of being wide-ranging in your mailing and sending to every single person on the list is to give you as many potential opportunities for work as possible.

If you send your material out to addresses in an old book, the chances are that a good percentage of those letters either will be undelivered, or will be thrown away by someone who can't be bothered to pass them on to his or her successor, or may come winging their way back to you. We want all your letters to arrive at the correct destination to have the maximum chance of getting you the one booking that as I've already said makes the whole of this exercise worth while. If you think it is an expensive exercise, then consider very carefully the cost of postage, the cost of the material which you are sending out; do a little financial exercise for yourself, and I think you will be agreeably surprised that by getting one, or possibly two major bookings, the cost of the exercise will have been completely covered, and from those bookings others may well result, return visits or build-on visits, as will be explained in a later chapter. Things really can snowball from year to year.

But for now, having told you what to send and where to send it, you need the rather crucial information of how and when.

6
The How and the When

You now have the material that you're going to send out and the names and addresses of the people that you want to send it to. So, what's next in the plan of campaign?

Envelopes
First of all you've got yourself some envelopes. A reminder: these envelopes must be of the right size to include whatever kind of brochure you have devised as a result of the advice in Chapter 4. Whether they should also include a letter or not we'll come to in a moment. But the important thing is that whatever you're sending out, you must pack it very, very carefully indeed. There is very little point in spending money on getting a brochure, on getting an envelope, on putting a stamp on that envelope, and addressing that envelope, if you don't make sure that what goes in the envelope is secure. If it bursts open in the post the chances of you ever seeing it again are pretty remote.

So how do you address the envelopes? If you have the energy to do it all yourself, or if you have a loving wife, or mother, or grandmother, or girl-friend, or lover, or if a group of you from college have clubbed together to be able to afford a secretary, then, as it were, you're laughing. If you don't have this facility, then you can go to a typing agency (here again you'll find the addresses in Yellow Pages), and you'll take along your envelopes or envelope labels, and you'll take along the *British Music Yearbook* or the other publications containing the lists of names and addresses, and the agency will type the addresses for you at a very reasonable cost. Very often, as some of you will know, they farm out this kind of work to young expectant mothers sitting at home, very keen to earn some extra pin money and very happy to do this light, easy kind of typing, that they can do either in between expecting the baby or in between feeds once the baby has arrived.

Letters

These typing agencies will also type for you as many copies of an identical letter as you require. If in fact you intend to send a duplicated letter, then my advice will be: no. A booker who receives a letter that is obviously duplicated, with a printed 'Dear' and a name written in at the beginning, and a scribbled signature at the end, will not be nearly as impressed as he or she might have been if an individually typed letter on your headed notepaper were included with your brochure. In your own handwriting you've topped it with 'Dear Mr X' and tailed with 'Yours sincerely' and your signature, and then it says in typing: 'I have pleasure in enclosing my brochure and hope very much that you will be able to offer me an engagement in your coming season. I look forward very much to hearing from you.' And if you live in the same district as the addressee, you can add in your own, I hope, fair hand that you would be pleased to come to see him to discuss possibilities.

If you do adopt this particular procedure, then please make sure that you do top and tail the letter by hand and that you do spell the recipient's name correctly from the lists in your possession. Recently, with my booker's hat on, I've received letters from young musicians well known to me, one of which began 'Dear' without the name being filled in (could they be being that affectionate?), another of which began 'Dear Sir or Madam' (they ought to know by now), and the third of which began with my name misspelt (and that I hate). Sympathetic as I am to the needs of young musicians, I am also, like all other bookers, human, and this kind of thing can turn you off that particular young musician if, in a similar mailing, you have just received a properly addressed letter and a decently printed and sent out brochure. And do check before sealing the envelopes in a mass mailing that you haven't put 'Dear Mr Pearcey' to someone you've known for years as Leonard – that sort of slip-up shows up alarmingly to the recipient.

I know one or two people who prefer to sign a different name at the end of the letters they send out with their mailings, pretending that they have a manager, so that it doesn't look as if they themselves are doing the actual touting for work. This can be perfectly acceptable as long as you remember what the other name is, and when somebody rings up and asks for that person you don't deny all knowledge of him or her. But better not – 'Oh what a tangled web we weave ...' and all that. If of course someone already established has the same name, you may have to change yours for professional reasons, but if not, and if your natural or maiden name is the one under which you have begun to get known, stick to it. Changing could mean starting again.

Timing

As to the when of this particular exercise, mailings should generally go out at the following times: for festivals – eighteen months before the festival date as given on the lists; for schools, universities, orchestras, Municipal Entertainment Officers, Regional Arts Associations, members of the National Federation of Music Societies – October/November for the following season, that is, twelve months in advance; for the others – as soon as you possibly can.

Here the important reminder is to plan your mailings well in advance. There is no point in deciding *in* October that you're going to write to all the members of the National Federation of Music Societies who might be able to offer you work, and then start trying to assemble your brochure and get the envelopes typed and so on, because the chances are if you're also practising and doing a certain amount of work, then by the time you've actually completed the whole exercise it'll be December or January, and many of the clubs will already have made up their minds. So, plan your time in such a way that you have everything ready at least a month before the date on which you intend to get it posted, your envelopes addressed or labelled, the stamps on, your brochure and your individually typed letter put inside, and the whole thing sealed up (self-sealing envelopes like self-adhesive labels are more expensive but save a lot of time). Don't seal them till shortly beforehand in case there's any 'stop-press' to go in.

If you are a young musician reading this at the end of an academic year before you go out into the big wide world, then if you start working now you will have everything ready by October. If you are a young musician at the beginning of your final academic year, then you are very well placed indeed and have plenty of time to get everything really adequately and thoroughly ready and planned out in your diary. All you then have to do is drop the envelopes into carrier bags, walk to the nearest post-box, pop them into its eager mouth and wish yourself the luck I'm wishing you at this moment.

7
The Booking Got

This is the imaginary interval where I assume that all your hard work in preparing this material and posting it off has resulted in you getting at least one booking.

Now I tell you what to do with it. 👉

8
Helping Those Who Book You

Diaries

As soon as the at-least-one booking has been offered to you, pencil the date into both your diaries. *Both* my diaries? you cry. Yes, *both* your diaries: the diary that goes with you everywhere you go, and the diary that stays permanently beside the telephone, a good big one this, with room for basic details of each engagement so that whoever answers the phone doesn't have to rummage through the files.

A pencilling is a booking that is only provisional. When the music club or festival director contacts you and asks if you're available on such and such a date, it's only a pencilling until they have been back to their committee and sent you an official letter of confirmation. A pencilling is put into your diary in pencil, a definite booking is put into your diary in ink. If you are offered a definite booking, and you already have a pencilling for someone else in your diary on that date, then you must ring that other person, who really has first right on you, and say, 'I have been offered a definite booking – are you in a position to confirm or not?' ('Yes,' cries the Bishop, his arms outstretched). If they are not in a position to confirm, then you must tell them reluctantly that you have a definite booking and that booking becomes definite in both your diaries. Keep diaries for reference in future years. And don't turn down a definite offer on the basis of a 'I'm sure we'll be confirming soon' vague promise from the original inquirer. Be firm.

Answering-Machines

Nothing is more frustrating both for an artist and for a potential booker than not being able to get in touch with that artist to make an inquiry, or once the booking has been pencilled not being able to make contact to confirm, or when confirmed not being able to get in touch by phone to sort out all the actual details of the engagement. Obviously you must be on the phone, but equally obviously you can't be expected to be sitting beside that phone every hour of the day and night. If you do not have the aforementioned loving mother, grandmother, wife, lover, son or daughter who's going to be by the phone permanently, then you must make arrangements to have the phone somehow or other always attended. There are various ways in which you can do this.

You can have calls to your number intercepted by the telephone exchange when you are out, if you make the arrangements in advance. For a small quarterly charge they will answer your phone when you tell them that you're going to be out, and refer the calls to another number. This other number could be a relation or it could be an answering-service. Addresses of answering-services and their telephone numbers are to be found in Yellow Pages. An answering-service will of course charge you for taking your messages; and in either case, when you return home you inform the telephone exchange that you are back, they cease to intercept your calls, and you then ring either your relative or the answering-service and get the messages that have come in, messages offering bookings sometimes, messages confirming bookings, messages asking for details about a booking that has been confirmed already. If the number you refer the calls to is on the same exchange as you then the calls can usually be diverted automatically.

An alternative to the intercept service is an answering-machine, and these come in varying degrees of sophistication. First of all there is the simple Post Office machine that will merely give a message to your callers saying that you are out and will they please call later or give them another number to phone. Or there is the machine that will actually take a message from your caller, and these messages you collect yourself when you are back at home. Or there is the most sophisticated machine of all that enables you to ring in from wherever you are in the country and collect the messages on the machine, perhaps leave a new message for your callers, or any other instructions which you may wish to dictate to the machine. This is invaluable on tour or for same-day booking offers.

Obviously an answering-machine can be an expensive item, but once again, believe me, its cost is paid for in bookings otherwise lost because a phone is unanswered. Unless somebody wants you very, very much indeed, after two or three attempts to get you and no reply, they will immediately then go and contact another artist with whom they *can* get in touch. And remember that music-club organisers, for example, being amateurs and probably therefore having a daytime job, tend to prefer to get in touch with non-agency artists in the evening, when all being well you'll actually be out on a job. This is another reason why you should definitely have an answering-machine, people don't just phone between the hours of 9 and 5. Of course, the fact that music-club organisers are generally anxious to make contact in the evening has an advantage as well: in that if you have to phone them it's cheap-rate time.

The only problem I've ever had with an answering-machine was due to a drunken friend who rang through and recorded most of Beethoven's Pastoral Symphony on my machine one night: I had to listen to the whole thing through when I got back very late just in case it was followed by an urgent message.

The other way that people will get in touch with you than by the telephone is of course by letter, and if you have moved, there are various precautions you must take here to help the people who have booked you. We've already touched on the question of little address stickers on your brochure and notepaper, so that you don't have to indulge in the expense of having a completely new set of brochures or notepaper printed as soon as you move. But a surprising number of people don't know that when you move, the Post Office, again for a small fee, will intercept letters sent to you at your old address and readdress them to your new place of abode. Similarly they will refer phone calls to your new number free of charge for a while, but if you move within the same exchange you can keep your old number by arrangement.

An Office System

If you are looking after your own life, dealing with your own phone calls and your own correspondence, then clearly you need a very simple office system. Let me suggest a very basic one which you can adapt to your own particular needs.

First of all, as far as phone calls are concerned, have a simple duplicate book, the kind that gives you a top copy, a carbon, and an undercopy, on numbered sheets – you can get them from your local stationers. Then every time you receive a phone call in connection with a booking or every time you make a phone call in connection with a booking, you put the date and time of that call in the duplicate book, and give brief details of the message and name of caller. For example, '3 p.m., 4 June, Mr X, Secretary of the Wimbledon Music Circle rang. Offered a booking for 12 December 19whatever (and remember it might be next year or the year after so get it right) at standard fee £x. I accepted and pencilled booking in diaries. He will phone back within a fortnight.'

When the message is complete you take the copy of the message and place it in a file, in a simple buff folder marked 'Bookings Pending' where you keep them in date order of the actual date of the engagement. Any other messages or correspondence that arise before the booking is confirmed you simply paperclip, or staple preferably, on to the original message, and as soon as the booking is confirmed you transfer it to another file which is 'Bookings Confirmed', where again it is kept in date order. Make sure the confirmation letter from the organiser confirms day, month and year, duration and starting time of performance (and rehearsal if applicable), programme, full address of hall, and fee. And looking ahead a leap, stick rigidly to what you agree. It's infuriating for organisers to print a programme and then have the artist announce something different or start late or underrun or turn up at the wrong hall a day late and a year early.

You should always reply to letters as promptly as possible, and again, if necessary using the same sheet of carbon paper that you have in your duplicate book, keep a copy of every letter you write, whether you write it by hand or whether, preferably, you type it. This is vitally important so that you are absolutely sure that you have given all the information necessary, you remember what fee you may have quoted, you know that on 12 June you confirmed the booking with the Wimbledon Music Circle Secretary. Once again, copies of all the letters that you write in connection with the confirmed booking will be stapled with the other correspondence relating to that engagement and kept in the file in date order of engagements.

Should you keep the correspondence once a booking is over? Certainly until your bill is paid, but thereafter really only the letter from the booker confirming the engagement, as it will include all the details plus a name and address (start a 'Bookings Completed' file), and also any thank-you letter you get from the organiser and from which with permission you can quote on future leaflets or brochures.

Another aspect of your basic office system should be a card index of all the works in your repertoire, giving publishers and the timings of the work. This is useful not only for programme-building, but also for the purposes of Performing Right Society returns. It is more than likely that you will be asked to complete such a return by the organisers of a concert, and on it you will have to indicate the title, composer and publisher of the works that you have performed in that particular concert or recital. It is also very useful on these cards to keep a note of the places and the dates when you performed those particular works. This is better than writing the details on the actual piece of music.

You should also keep a file which contains the programmes of all the recitals and concerts that you give. These again should be kept in date order and include encores. This will be invaluable should you be invited back to a particular club, as you can instantly know what you performed before. It is also useful to write on the programmes what you actually wore (this applies to men as well as women) so that you know the standard of dress to be expected next time and so that you can make sure that you don't wear exactly the same dress next time – and it is also very useful to add the name, address and telephone number of the person you stayed with if you were given private hospitality.

The final aspect of your office system for now is your invoicing system, and again in the early stages a simple duplicate book will be sufficient. It is usually most convenient if you write out the invoice for any particular engagement and take it with you and hand it to the organisers on the night. This of course is if you are booked direct and not through an agent. You should regularly check through the copy invoices left in the book, and as soon as you have been paid for an engagement, mark it very clearly as having been paid, but make sure you take the carbon paper out first so that 'Paid' doesn't appear on an unpaid one as well. Then should you not be paid within a month you are perfectly within your rights to approach the organisers and ask why the cheque has not been sent, although usually it is best to arrange for the cheque to be handed over on the night in exchange for your invoice. Remember though that the wheels of big organisations like, for example, local authorities grind exceeding slow. If you haven't been paid after three months, see your solicitor or professional organisation (more on these later).

If you find that you are getting very, very busy, and that it would be better for you to have a secretary but you can't afford to have one on your own, then it may be, as already suggested, that one or two of your friends in a similar position will club together with you and you'll be able to afford to have a secretary jointly, say, for one or two mornings a week.

Admin Sheet
Even if you do have a secretary you may find it very convenient to devise your version of what I call my Admin Sheet. It covers most of the essential points in connection with any forthcoming visit, and it is my custom to send it to bookers approximately two months before I'm due to appear for them. When I have entered the confirmed date in my diary, then two months beforehand I mark in

'Send Admin Sheet to ...' followed by the name of the organisation.

My Admin Sheet covers the following points, and is a simple duplicated sheet so that I don't have to type it out every single time:

Arrival
'Unless I hear from you to the contrary I will arrive about an hour before the time I am due to start to try the hall. As I will be coming by car, I would appreciate a route for finding you and a reserved parking space if necessary.'

A few words of explanation here. Clearly, if you are going to be staying with somebody overnight and they would like you to arrive beforehand to change, or if you want a full rehearsal, then they will make special arrangements when they reply to you. As far as getting a route is concerned, don't be convinced if the organiser writes back and says, 'Don't worry, you can't go wrong, anyone will tell you the way', because, believe me, you can and they won't. There is nothing worse than arriving in a car, driving yourself, alone, on a very wet, possibly foggy night, looking for local inhabitants to tell you the way to the Memorial Hall, and finding nobody at all, or if you do find anybody, discovering that they haven't got a clue where the Memorial Hall is. And still ask for a route if you've been before: one-way systems have a habit of changing or popping up overnight.

David Jacobs tells a lovely 'Any Questions?' story on this line in one of his excellent lectures, about the time when he came out of the hotel where the pre-broadcast dinner was being held, leapt into the provided car and said, 'To the hall, please'; and the driver turned round and said, 'Which hall, Mr Jacobs?', and David said, 'Haven't you been told?', and the driver said, 'No', and David realised that he himself didn't know so he rushed back into the hotel, grabbed a copy of *Radio Times*, looked at the 'Any Questions?' billing, found out the name of the hall which was printed in those days, charged back out, got into the car, gave the name of the hall to the driver, and off they went. But it wasn't till he got to the hall and was waiting for the team to arrive from the same hotel that he realised that they wouldn't know either and they might not put two and two together and turn to the *Radio Times* if their driver hadn't got a clue where to go, and he was absolutely right. They eventually got there slightly late, but it must have been an emotional experience all round.

The bit about the reserved parking space, although it may sound a little arrogant, is again an essentially practical point: if you arrive, ladies, with your hair beautifully done, and you've forgotten an umbrella, and it's absolutely pouring with rain, then the last thing you want to have to do is stagger half a mile across the car park with your harp.

Publicity

'I enclose some photographs, press cuttings and biographies which you may find useful in any publicity you may be planning for local press, radio, TV and the like. Let me know if you would like more copies of anything for these purposes. If possible please return the photos when you have finished with them.'

Even if they are reproductions rather than original prints, they still cost money and they aren't really much use to the local press after they have finished with them so you might as well have them back for further use. It helps if you put your little address sticker on the back and write 'Please return to'. But do make sure that the ink is dry before you pack the photos together.

There will be the occasional organisers who will take great exception to this particular paragraph, feeling that it insinuates that they don't know how to run their music club when in fact they know perfectly well about sending pictures and little news stories to local newspapers to get publicity for the engagement for which they've booked you. However, 99 times out of 100, people are absolutely delighted with this kind of help and, of course, like all the two-way traffic ideas that we've mentioned, not only does it help the music club and the event for which they are forking out for your fee, it also gives you further publicity and may lead to further bookings in the future. Clearly, you are offering this publicity material for free.

Equipment

As I offer an evening of songs with guitar, my paragraph here simply says: 'All I need on the platform is a high stool to sit on. The setting out of the seating and performing areas should please be as informal as possible.'

If you, for example, are a string quartet then you should suggest four chairs and four music stands, if necessary; if you are a pianist, and although this may seem ridiculous it has been shown to be necessary, you should point out that there should be a piano and that it should be in tune. And so on. This particular paragraph should, of course, be written as politely as possible.

Programme and Programme Notes

The question of the content of your programme will be dealt with in the next chapter but the important question of sending the organisers full details of what

... the last thing you want to have to do
is stagger half a mile across the car park with your harp

you intend to sing or play together with programme notes if they so desire, comes in this particular section. Only send programme notes written by somebody else if you have permission or if you have paid the necessary copyright fees.

Hospitality

The question of hospitality is usually best dealt with in the brief letter that will accompany your admin sheet and the press kit that it includes. It is very important if you happen to be allergic to budgies or if you are a vegetarian, and if you are due to accept private hospitality, to let the organisers know this so that they do not put you with the keeper of a large aviary who only eats meat.

Again, if you are travelling by train and accepting private hospitality, or even if you are staying at a hotel, don't accept being told that the hotel or the house is only just two or three minutes' walk from the station. If you arrive with a double-bass and it's snowing a blizzard, it's much nicer to be met, and most organisers will respond to this request and bring their own car if asked politely.

If you do plan to stay in a hotel or if a hotel room is part of the agreed contract, then make absolutely sure that you know whether it is your responsibility to book the room and then claim the expenses back on your invoice, or if the room is being booked by the local organisers and they are paying, with the bill being forwarded to them by the hotel for payment. Clearly this latter alternative is preferable, but don't run up transatlantic phone bills and then waltz off first thing after breakfast leaving them to pick up an inflated tab. Whichever the alternative, the arrangements must be confirmed in a letter to the hotel.

Final Note on This Chapter

Although this chapter is called 'Helping Those Who Book You', you'll be well aware that one or two of the things are very much self-interest from your point of view. Similarly, in the next chapter there is an overlap, even though it's called 'Helping Yourself'. But another plea: even when you have an agent, don't off-load these responsibilities.

9

Helping Yourself

And if you think the title of this chapter sounds a bit like self-service, well, you're absolutely right: serve yourself, look after yourself. Just as the previous chapter has given an indication of how to serve the people who offer you the bookings, so you must also serve yourself well, service yourself.

Right at the start of this book I mentioned that some things are going to seem terribly obvious, and this is just one of those chapters, because I'm going to be talking about the way you dress, the way you do your hair, the way you behave. Don't think it's something so terribly basic that therefore you know all about it, because you don't, as reading on is about to tell you.

Let's start with something not quite so basic, the question of programming.

Programming

I hope this is something that you will have been taught within the walls of your music college: how to put a balanced programme together, how to consider different feelings, different moods, different styles, different colours, different keys. Always programme well within your own limitations: don't add new works until you're completely confident in them, and don't add too much that's new on one date if you can avoid it.

Remember the advice given earlier in this book, about only having works in your repertoire that you can play at the drop of a hat. There may be works that you think you can play at the drop of a hat that are in fact beyond you, and it will serve neither you nor your bookers well if you include one of those in your programme. Study the market, see what your friends or competitors or rivals or colleagues in the business may be playing. Clearly you don't want to be offering exactly the same programme as someone who's very similar to you in style and artistry, but at the same time you don't want to go 'over the top' in trying to be absolutely different from that particular person.

And take very much into account the type of performance that you are being asked to give, the occasion on which the concert is being held, the kind of audience that will be sitting in front of you. Very often the organisers of, say, a music club will give you a very clear outline of the type of programme that they require. But sometimes they leave the choice up to you. You should then get a fairly clear idea from the organisers of the sort of people they expect to turn up and programme with those people in mind. Don't play a vastly complicated, difficult-to-follow, modern programme if you're going to be faced with an audience of very young schoolchildren. Similarly, don't play a vastly overcomplicated programme if the purpose of the occasion is to entertain a general audience, or even an audience perhaps of non music-lovers. The key is, study your market, programme within your limitations, and above all programme music you feel for and know about.

Dress

But now I'm afraid it really is down to the basics of the way you dress, your hair, your behaviour, and don't think that this question of the way you dress refers only to the female sex. I still remember vividly having booked a very promising young string quartet for a concert in the Merton Festival, and sitting in the front row with them on a raised platform in front of me, being absolutely fascinated first of all by the state of their shoes and secondly by the fact that they were wearing violently coloured, diamond-patterned socks with their white tie and tails. They played beautifully, and of that there is no doubt at all, but the state of their tailcoats and the lack of creases in their trousers gave rise to a fair number of comments. O.K., you could argue that I was the organiser, sitting at the front, and should have been concentrating only on their musical talents, but unfortunately one is distracted by dirty shoes, by crumpled clothes, if you like. Remember that audiences don't glance, they stare for up to two hours at a time, and that's why things get out of proportion.

It is vital that you should at all times be well turned out. Always check, men, to find out what the organisers want you to wear, whether they want you to wear white tie, black tie, lounge suit, whatever it may be. Sometimes they may want you to dress informally in slacks and a pullover but watch it if you have heavy underarm perspiration like some TV conductors. Always check, and whatever they

64

want, go on stage as well turned out in that particular style of outfit as you possibly can be. Don't travel to or from an engagement in any of your performance outfits, change when you get there and before you leave, in the changing-room/green-room that should always be provided. A suit or dress carrier, a same-day cleaner and an iron, should be featured in your philosophy, and on tour spray dry-clean, sewing and shoe-cleaning kits.

It may be that when you are very, very famous indeed, and have developed a reputation for having a striking and original personality, then you can go along in filthy jeans with a fag hanging out of the side of your mouth. But unfortunately people do tend to judge the professional standard of singing or playing by the image that a person portrays, and if the image is slovenly, and this includes the way you dress at rehearsals as well as performances, then it is likely that your overall reputation will be judged to be slovenly as well. Once in those far distant Baccholian student days we arrived at our smart hotel scruffily dressed and sticky after a long car journey, and were ordered round to the back entrance before we could explain we were guests.

But why bother about the way you dress at rehearsals? Apart from the above, the answer is because you never know what's going to happen at a rehearsal. Somebody may come rushing in and say, 'Is there anybody here who can come instantly to sing such and such a work in such and such a place', your agent may ring and ask you to go straight on to an audition, or it may be that you are in a recording studio and the producer says, 'I'm going to an important reception this evening, I'd very much like you to come with me', and in this case it's you that goes, not the piano or violin, so you and your talent are reflected in your appearance alone. If you are well dressed, even casually and comfortably so, then you can take advantage of every opportunity that may present itself.

As far as dress for young ladies is concerned, I can do no better than start this particular paragraph with what is one of my favourite stories of all time, told by Lady Barbirolli, Evelyn Rothwell, the distinguished oboist who has attended more of the seminars that I have given on the subject of advice for young musicians than any other performer, and whose assistance and guidance and support have been invaluable. She tells this marvellous story of attending a party after a recital which was a return visit to this particular organisation, and two of the lady members of the committee came up to her and said, 'Lady Barbirolli, we're so glad that you wore that beautiful dress ... again.'

I did suggest, ladies, in an earlier chapter, that you keep a note in your

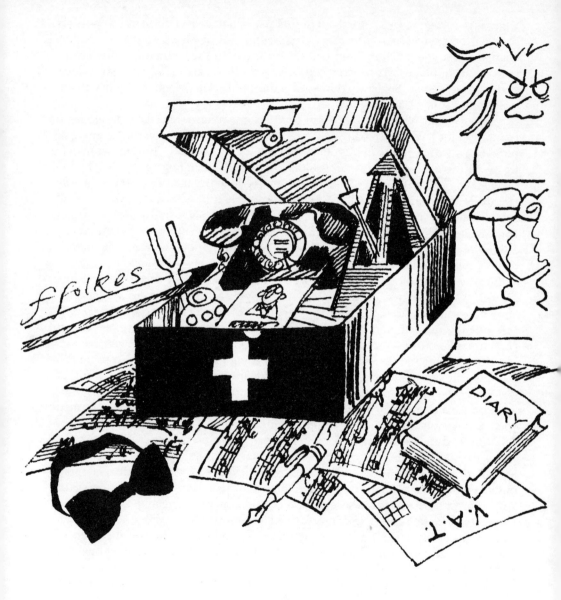

programme file not only of the programmes that you gave but also of what you wore at any particular club. If you are one of a group of soloists, then you should consult with the other ladies to make sure that the colours of your dresses aren't going to clash; you should also find out what colour the curtains in the hall are going to be or the 'uniform' dresses of the choir ladies, so that your dress doesn't clash with them either or, even worse, if they're the same colour, that you don't disappear into nothingness. And dresses should never be too fussy, with too much detail: apart from the fact that detail will often be lost from the back of a large hall, fussy detail can detract just as much from a performance as soup stains. Make sure also that your dresses travel well and are comfortable.

Make-up and Personal Hygiene
Being neither a beautician nor your best friend, I'm leaving this one to your good sense. But ladies, do have professional make-up advice to make the most of yourself on stage; men, do have a portable razor for a pre-show polish-up; and both, keep a toilet bag permanently stocked for travelling.

Hair
And your hair. A hair style is vitally important to a performer who is going to be speaking or singing and whose eyes are therefore going to come into play. The lighting even in some leading halls is often as bad as it can be in some little provincial church halls, so in rehearsal find the best-lit position for you; if you have a style that is forward over your eyes, and the lighting is bad, a shadow will be cast on your face, and the audience does love to see a performer's face, especially when that performer is speaking or singing and therefore the eyes are backing up what the mouth is uttering.

Behaviour
In connection with that Lady Barbirolli story just now, I mentioned the fact that she was attending a little party, a little reception, after her concert. The importance of socialising cannot be overstressed. Both for professional and amateur organisers, meeting the performer, getting to know the performer, even very briefly, is as much part of the adventure of the booking as the actual performance. Here you can serve yourself as well as serving the people who book you.

If you say that you're going to arrive at a certain time, then arrive at that time, or earlier if possible. If it is your custom to be private and still and quiet before a recital and during the interval, then fair enough. But do at least say 'Good evening', 'Hello' to the organisers. O.K., making music *is* a business, you *are* earning your living, but it is a business that depends very much on your own individual personality, quiet or extrovert, as well as your performing ability, and as an organiser it is good to be greeted, and at the end of the day to be thanked, for that particular engagement, whether it be by a thank-you letter, or a thank-you in person, or a bunch of flowers if the organiser is a lady, remembering thank-yous to those who provided hospitality as well.

Socialising

If you're not the kind of person who likes to be quiet during the interval, and I fall into the category of someone who *doesn't* like to be quiet during the interval, then go out and mix with the audience if they're having coffee, or go and talk to some of the children in the hall, and talk to them from the stage as much as you possibly can. Some performers score by saying goodbye at the door to the audience as it leaves. In schools concerts a question time is a good idea. You usually get the same first three: 'How old are you?', 'How many children have you got?', 'Are you married?' (in that order), and I'm always glad of my ad-libbing ability with kids, especially when after a big intro, an hour of songs and stories, and a tremendous round of applause, you end question time by saying, 'Time for just one more', and from a six-year-old you get, 'Please sir, who are you?'

But even here there has to be a major warning: in your contact, in your socialising, behave *well*. I remember that after sending out one girl student from the Guildhall School of Music and Drama to do solo engagements, organisers began ringing me up and saying, 'Mr Pearcey, whatever you do, don't send that girl again. She thinks she's a prima donna. AND she treats us like dirt.' Remember that if you do treat people like dirt, or if you ignore them, or if you are scruffy, then those organisers, at whatever level they may be, those top professional festival directors or those amateur local small-society lady organisers, meet up with colleagues in the same league, and they will discuss you, and they will say, 'Whatever you do, don't book that girl, because she thinks she's the best thing since sliced bread, and treats everybody like dirt. O.K., she sings beautifully, but so does so-and-so, and she's a nice girl to have around.'

I'm lucky, because I enjoy meeting people and being with them. I always regret the fact that, except on return bookings, you hardly ever see the good friends you make on engagements again, because next time you're near them your loyalty is to someone else, some other organiser. In the early Baccholian Singers days the rest of the quintet left the socialising to me and made a bridge four. And, contrary to what I've been saying, it became an affectionate talking-point that they always got out the cards. So perhaps if you do go off bird-watching or dowsing instead of socialising it'll add to your image and make people want you even more. Remember Garbo.

Deportment

That mention of Baccholian Singers reminded me of another important heading. At our Wigmore début, which was highly successful, someone told us we walked on and off like weary furniture-removers (echoes of that livery dinner in Chapter 1). Always come on and go off stage with style, acknowledge applause properly, and if encores is your policy, know what you're going to do and announce it. But having given them more than their pound of flesh, quit while you're winning and leave them wanting more.

Word of Mouth

The advice in this book is designed to help *you* to make your career, to get work, as well as designed to help you to help the people who give you that work, but one of the most potent factors in the development of your career is your reputation as it goes round by word of mouth. Organisers are hardly likely to write in a newspaper to say how dreadfully you behaved, but they are quite likely to tell each other in informal conversation. And after all, all these points about dress, hair, behaviour, socialising, in fact the way you present your programme and yourself, the kind of image that you have got, are so basic: because the person who takes trouble all the way down the line, who makes sure that the programme is well put together and well performed, who takes the trouble to dress well, who takes the trouble to arrive on time, to be a perfect guest as well as a good performer, well, that's the person who's going to score all the way down the line and get a much greater quantity of work. But don't be phoney – let all this come naturally.

Fee Negotiation

At this point in this chapter we take a slightly sideways jump, because the question of fee negotiation comes into the question of helping yourself. The whole problem of fees again is dealt with in a later chapter, but this is a little piece of advice as to whether you should negotiate on your fee or not.

Let us assume that you have fixed your fee at a certain level, as outlined in the subsequent chapter in this book, and a music-club organiser, for good reasons or bad, asks you if you are prepared to come for less than that fee. My advice, and the advice of many other professional colleagues, would be to say, 'No'. Once you have established yourself at a certain level on the music-fee scale, stay at that level. There are younger performers than yourself at the start of a career who might go for the reduced fee at which you are being asked to perform, because that is the fee level at which they have started themselves anyway; and you will find that if you do drop your fee, you are somehow devaluing the currency. If you're asked to go somewhere for nothing to play for charity, then that of course is a different thing. But somehow it works out, every time, that if people think they can get you for a cheaper price than you actually advertise, then somehow they seem to feel that you're not quite up to being what you're cracked up to be, and the way they treat you, and their attitude towards you, changes. And if you go to one club for less than you charge a neighbouring club, you're asking for trouble.

I remember I was approached, when I was Music Director of the Guildhall School of Music and Drama, by the organiser of a music club who had given a lot of good engagements to a lot of good students, and therefore to whom I was extremely grateful; and he asked me if I would go down to the West Country to give a special concert for his music club. He felt that the kind of evening of songs with guitar that I offered was just right for reviving what was seeming to be a slightly flagging membership, but he pointed out that he could only afford to pay me at the kind of rates at which he had paid the students.

Although I had a firm rule, based on bitter experience, that I would never ever go anywhere for a reduced fee – either full fee, or nothing for charity – in this particular case, out of loyalty to the students, I accepted. I travelled down there on a very wet and very windy day, and reported to his house at the time requested. I waited for an hour, and he didn't turn up; so I went to his offices in the town, which were closed. I then went to the concert hall, where I was informed that he was on an extended holiday. He was due back, but had decided not to come back.

So I went and found a restaurant, and gave myself the meal he had agreed to give me, then went back to the hall and waited for someone to come to tell me what the plan of the evening was going to be, but nobody came. Then at half past seven there was evidently an audience in the hall, so I went out, gave the first part of the recital, which went well, came back in the interval, gave the second part which also went well, at the end of which a lady stood up having had almost two hours of songs with guitar, and thanked me for one of the best violin recitals she had ever attended. I then retired to the hotel room that I'd had to book for myself. And I never even got a proper apology. The argument here could be that I was there to perform for the audience, and therefore the way the organiser behaves doesn't matter. But I tell you the story because it does indicate what other professionals will confirm, and that is, what happens if you reduce your fee and devalue your own particular currency. Another quote from Guildhall days: 'They ought to be happy to come for nowt if we put their names on the posters' – WRONG!

Delays

It also points up one or two other factors. Whenever you go anywhere, take with you all the correspondence relating to that particular booking. You never know when your memory might fail you if you only think you've remembered the hall you're supposed to be performing at, or if you think you've remembered the address of the organiser. Always take with you all the information you've got, including the organiser's telephone number and, if possible, the hall telephone number.

Then if by any chance your car breaks down or you are involved in an accident through no fault of your own, you are able to send a message through to that hall to let the very worried organiser know that you are going to be, perhaps, half an hour late. Then at least, the organiser can advise the audience, and everybody knows that you are actually turning up. There really is nothing worse than being an organiser who doesn't know whether the artist is going to turn up or not. If you're travelling by train the chances are that if the train has been delayed the organiser will find that out from the station, but even so you should take all the information with you in case you need to make a quick phone call when you arrive at the station.

Travelling

The rigours of travelling point up another factor of course, and that is, your actual state of health and your state of peace of mind when you step on to that concert platform. Some performers do try to take on too much work, or do try to get the maximum out of their life by limiting their travelling time and limiting the time that they regard as being wasted between arriving and walking on to the stage. This is another false economy. Arrive in good time to relax, to meet the organisers, to get organised yourself. Don't overstretch yourself, don't drive if it's a long distance and a train journey would in fact be much less tiring. Don't drive in order to save money if you've been offered first-class rail expenses and you think the petrol would be cheaper. If it's a very long way, and you haven't, say, three other quartet members to share the driving, then you will arrive tired and you will be affecting your state of health and performance.

Health

A certain basic exercise routine every morning is invaluable to every performer. If you're a fiddle player or pianist the chances are that you do particular finger exercises anyway, and obviously if you're a singer you do vocal exercises.

But I'm talking really about the battle of the bulge. Magazines are very good at coming forward with basic keep-fit routines for men and women: find the one that suits you and do it every morning. If, as I hope, you're already practising for several hours each day to keep up your high musical standard, a few more minutes of your time spent on an exercise routine will hardly be missed. The state of your health is reflected in the way you look, it's reflected in your hair, it's reflected in your attitude, and if you are in good health and if you look after yourself, when it comes to work load and to travelling, then not only will you have a longer working life, but you will give better performances.

You'll know by now also that there's nothing worse for you and the audience than a very cold hall (except perhaps a very hot one). If a recalcitrant caretaker is to blame there's not much you can do about it, but Louis Kentner told me that Dame Myra Hess had told him about once having to play the Schumann Concerto in her cardigan, though she took it off for the cadenza. Following which story, Griselda Kentner remembered the occasion when her husband couldn't understand the laughter as he began the Wanderer Fantasy, hardly a humorous piece, on an American tour until he realised that he was still wearing his large white galoshes, reminiscent apparently of vast contraceptives. Exit, remove galoshes, and Louis Kentner returns to a rapturous round of applause.

Talking again about coldness, some years ago I gave a recital in the dead of a snowy winter in a little town miles from anywhere and I stayed with the bank manager in his flat over the bank. He and his wife were the kindest of people but the warmth of their hospitality was matched by the coldness of the bedroom they gave me: their absent son must have been a real anti-heat freak. Anyway, in the early hours of the morning I decided to call it a night, and drive back to London – I'd said I might leave early as it was quite a drive and there wasn't a suitably timed

A certain basic exercise routine every morning
is invaluable to every performer

train. So I dressed, left a note of thanks, and slipped out of the flat past the amiable black labrador, and slammed the flat door behind me.

Down the stairs to the front door – and I'd forgotten it was a bank. Security locks and bars everywhere. Locked in front, locked behind, imagine your hero's predicament. And still five hours to go till opening time. All I could do was go back to the flat and ring the bell. Loud threatening barking from the ferocious black labrador and eventually a sleepy bank manager (was that a gun in his dressing-gown pocket?), 'Oh it's you Leonard, you're back, come on in.' Quite where he thought I'd been on the razzle I don't know, the nearest thing they'd had to night life in the town for quite some time was my recital. Embarrassed explanation that I was trying to get out not in; and so to London.

Non-musical Publicity

The for-example here is another little personal story, relevant this time, designed to illustrate the value of keeping your name before the public as much as you possibly can. I've already discussed the question of music publicity, of sending information that can be used in the local or national press, and getting yourself on to radio and television, and there's more to come on this particular theme, but it's always worth remembering that the people who book you also read non-specialist areas of their newspapers and magazines, and if anything happens to you that is of any interest at all outside your direct musical performance, if for example you marry a princess or if for example you win some particular bravery award, then let the press know about it. It's two-way traffic with journalists, as well.

My example concerns a day when I left the Guildhall School of Music and Drama to go and give an evening recital not far out of London. I'd taken the car up to town, but I kept the guitar in my office for safety. I took it down to the car, put it on the roof of the car, unlocked the door, got in, and drove off happily over Blackfriars Bridge. Crossing the bridge I heard a thump and wondered what it was but didn't think anything of it, but it wasn't until I was over the other side of the bridge that I realised what I'd done: left the guitar on the roof of the car and it had fallen off.

Immediately I turned the car round and drove back, expecting to see the case and guitar a crumpled mass under the wheels of some juggernaut. But no, there was a policeman standing holding my guitar, in its case, while the homegoing London business crowds were greeting him with jocular cries of, 'Give us a song, Officer', and other such ribald remarks. What had happened was that a kind motorist driving almost immediately behind me had seen what had occurred, had stopped his car, got out in the middle of the heavy, rush-hour traffic, rescued my guitar, and handed it to the policeman standing by.

Somehow I had to find a way of thanking that gentleman, so I rang both the London evening newspapers first thing the following morning, and gave them the story. It was printed, and I hope very much that my homegoing London motorist read one of the London evenings and would therefore have seen how grateful I was to him for what he had done to save my guitar. But it had a side effect: someone read the story who was looking for an artist to come and give a private evening of songs with guitar, and I was the artist that he booked.

Credit Where Credit's Due

By phoning through to the London evenings, I'd given them a good little story, but also I'd said thank you to that motorist, just as I advise you to say thank you to music-club organisers, and to give credit where credit is due. If you have been helped in your career by a scholarship, or by a début recital series, or by an individual person, or by an arts organisation, always as often as possible give credit to the individual or organisation concerned.

Similarly, if anything goes wrong in your planning, in your arrangements, always be ready to apologise: apologies disarm, apologies help, apologies flatter to a certain extent. And they do show you care. They can even help when you're in the right.

And finally, on this theme of helping yourself, don't be worried if you are not an extrovert who enjoys socialising and the like. Do make the effort, even if you are shy. It will be genuinely appreciated.

10
Building on the Booking

Let's imagine again that you have got this one booking, as the result of the extensive mailing that you have undertaken. How can you build on it, how can you make the most out of it? Once again let me tell you about the system that I adopted at the outset of my career. A simple one, but again a very effective one.

A System
I had a large map on which I marked all the major festivals, all the major music clubs, and the major television and radio stations. Then whenever I got a booking (in your case let's imagine it's this one-off booking) I would pinpoint that on the map, and then see which major festivals, music clubs, radio and television stations were near by. Then I would write to them again. O.K., they would have been covered as part of the initial mailing that got me that one booking, but this would be a reminder, it would be a follow-up, and it would be a special letter, again enclosing my brochure and any other relevant or new publicity material, but this time also telling them about this one booking. Now we'll assume further in your case that it is an evening music-club booking.

You will write, for example, to the major festivals and other major music clubs in the area, and say, 'On the evening of such and such a date at such and such a time I have been engaged to give a recital for the so-and-so music club. I hope very much that you will be able to attend. If so, please let me know and I will arrange for you to receive tickets,' Offer them tickets (always two, remember, and free), but don't send them tickets until they indicate that they are prepared to attend. This is two-way traffic too: it's in their interests to know who's around and their reputations zoom if they always book the best going.

76

Obviously, you must consult with the organiser of the booking that you have got on the best way of issuing tickets: it may be that they will be left at the door for them, it may be that you will have tickets sent to you to forward on to the festival directors or music-club organisers who accept, but the important point is not to send the tickets out until you actually have a definite acceptance. And when you do send them out, ask the recipients to return them if by any chance they aren't able to come, just in case, as we hope may happen, you have a sell-out and all unused tickets can be resold. People return unwanted tickets much more readily if they've asked for them in the first place: unsolicited and unwanted tickets tend to go into the bin. And remember you may have to pay for those tickets.

You should make a point of meeting (so that they can meet you) the organisers or directors who do turn up at your invitation to thank them for coming; and if you get a friendly reply that they aren't free that evening see if they will let you call to see them when you're in the area.

As far as the radio and television stations are concerned, write and give them the same information, and say that you will be happy to call in and record some items for them, or perform live in the context of a programme that's going out, or even be prepared to be interviewed in a news or magazine programme. Here again it's always a case of a two-way traffic: regional news and magazine programmes on radio and television are in my experience always delighted to learn of a possible musical item and musical interview. Not only again does it help you, it helps the radio and television producers, and it also helps the event that you are performing in by giving it extra and indirect publicity.

Tours

But this building on the booking isn't only about encouraging people to come and hear or see you, or getting yourselves on radio or television. It is also about getting other bookings to tie in with that one and making, if you like, a small tour. We've assumed that the booking that you've got is an evening booking with a music club. Well, by using again the *British Music Yearbook* and *Music Education Handbook*, and referring to your map, find out, for example, what lunch-time performance opportunities there may be in the area. Write to the Schools Music Adviser and say that you're going to be in his area on such and such a date giving an evening performance, and you'd be delighted to perform for schools during the day.

See if the local arts associations know of any opportunities for definite bookings while you're in the area, or if the Municipal Entertainment Officers are perhaps organising a series of lunch-time concerts round about that time because it's the summer and lots of tourists are going to be there, and they'll be delighted to learn that you're actually going to be in the area already. Try the local public or private schools and nearby universities, in fact try everybody in the various categories listed in Chapter 5 in this book.

The fact that you are already in the area with, if you've handled things correctly, your expenses being paid, means that you can offer an engagement for your normal fee, but also with reduced expenses. It would be very bad politically to say, 'As my expenses are already being paid I can come to you for no expenses and just the fee.' That would certainly make it very much cheaper for the additional bookers who come to you, but would be highly unfair to the original booker, thanks to whose generosity in giving you the engagement in the first place you are able to build up this mini-tour.

The correct thing to do is to split the expenses between the various bookings that you end up with. This reduction of expenses to the original booker is one good way of saying thank you for taking the risk and having faith in you.

With luck, you will find yourself with a plan that might go something like this: your original booking was on, say, a Tuesday evening. On the Tuesday morning you could give some concerts in a local primary school, at lunch-time a recital for the Municipal Entertainment Officer, some more schools concerts in the afternoon, a visit to the television studio or the radio studio at tea-time, then a rest before your evening performance, with possibly some more schools concerts the following day and an extra music-club performance the following evening before you return to base on the third day.

The Original Booker

This kind of special mailing has always, in my experience, worked out extremely well. It should be undertaken immediately you have confirmation of the one booking on which you plan to base this mini-tour, but please remember to keep the original booker in the picture. If by any chance that booker knows that the music clubs you intend to approach have similar audiences to his own, and would detract from the audience for his performance, then he would have every right to say, 'I would prefer you didn't approach that particular music club'; sometimes in fact, notably in public halls, your contract will include a clause that prevents you from performing within a certain radius for a specific time just because of this audience-clash reason.

But usually organisers in one area will have good contacts with other clubs where there will be no clash, will know the local music adviser, will know the music producers in the local radio and television stations, and will be only too glad to help you, because in helping you they will be helping themselves and their society.

A Good Example

And if you think that you've got through one chapter without having a for-example story, then I'm afraid you're wrong. My favourite story in this field concerns a very distinguished singer, an extremely good friend of mine, Maureen Lehane, who some years ago now, although very successful in this country, had never managed to break into any kind of performing career in the U.S.A. Then one day along came just one very well-paid booking, with all expenses, in the States.

Instead of doing what perhaps many other people would have done, and what perhaps initially you might have been tempted to do, go to the States, sing, grab the large fee and come straight back, she used that money to travel round America auditioning for as many leading conductors, orchestras and the like as she possibly could. She came back to this country without the large fee, but with a large string of bookings, and now returns to the United States regularly two or three times a year.

En Route Bookings

The plan that has been suggested in this chapter is for building up a clump of engagements in one particular area. I mustn't forget the other angle, and that is the *en route* booking. Let's assume for example that you have obtained a booking in the North of Scotland, or the North of England, or the North of Wales come to that. This particular exercise involves a little more thought and a little more effort than the immediate-area booking: often it is possible to arrange a series of bookings on your way to the far-distant one. The principle involved is exactly the same: writing, notifying, offering, and spreading expenses, except that rather than concentrating on the particular area you concentrate, if you like, on clubs, festivals, radio and television stations, and so on, along the line of the proposed route by car or by train to and from your booking in the North.

If you do both the *en route* build-up *and* the clump build-up, then you've really made good use of the one initial booking.

11
Building on the Investment
1: Further Self-Promotion

You've now spent time and money on launching your career. How can you build on that investment?

Annual Mailings

Once you've started your mailing system it's important and useful to keep it going every year. As you update your brochure with new photographs, new press notices, new repertoire items, more impressive engagements, and, I hope, a slightly higher fee, so you will have more to tell your prospective bookers. Someone who may not have been impressed with what you said the first time round will see that you are now developing in your career and have become someone well worth booking. The snowball effect really does work and the more work you get the more you are likely to be in demand.

One year, before I had an agent to include me in her mailings, I suddenly couldn't face the amount of work involved, so decided not to do the mailing at all. I discovered later that a lot of people thought that I'd given up my evenings of songs with guitar. The lesson here: unless you have an agent to do it for you, keep the mailings going yourself, otherwise you undo the good that you have done, and will not be making the most of your original investment of time and money. Some years ago I got one of the bookings I'd been longing to get ever since I started my mailings, and I learned from the organiser, through correspondence, that he'd actually given me the booking because he admired my persistence. You can never tell for what reason your efforts will be rewarded.

And don't ignore people who have already booked you. Let's hope you were so good that they will long to have you back again, perhaps after a year or so, but if they don't receive your material in the post each year, they may well forget you. It is a sad fact that the information in front of a booker at any one time may supersede memories of a past success: out of sight, out of mind, and all that. So keep *your* name to the fore. The elements of chance and of being 'in the right place at the right time' (self or brochure) play a part here too. Similarly your individual mailing can have more impact with its one brochure than a mass mailing of brochures or lists from an agency, though remember that some bookers prefer dealing with an agency because of the risk of cancellation (q.v.).

Never in your annual mailings send out the same brochure as before if you don't have any updating material to go with it. Bookers who merely receive exactly the same mailing as they received the year before, or possibly two years before, will not be particularly impressed. Another advantage of having a new brochure printed each year with an updated fee on it echoes back to my consolation advice that if you didn't receive an immediate return to every single letter you shouldn't think that that letter has fallen on stony ground. It may have been, you will recall, that the booker has decided to keep the letter and refer to it on some future occasion when he is in a position to book you. But by that time your fee may well have changed, so the existence of a new brochure with a new fee (and we've discussed putting your fee on your brochure), that can be sent out immediately to an inquirer, will ensure that you don't have to work for the old fee and save you having to argue it out on the phone.

Self-Assessment

But there's a little caveat that doesn't quite belong under any other heading, which seems to fit quite nicely in here: sometimes it's very difficult to judge just how successful you have been. The best way I can illustrate this is to give a for-example from my own experience: my evening of songs with guitar can be very light, and from time to time the committee of a music club, I have learned later, although they normally were very keen, say, on Bartók String Quartets, have felt that their membership would really in fact enjoy a much lighter concert, and have booked me almost in spite of themselves to give one of my lighter evenings. The audience have enjoyed it hugely, the committee have sat around rather like schoolteachers who don't quite approve of their children eating sweets but know that the children enjoy it so allow them to do it and actually enjoy themselves too.

Similarly you may go down like a bomb with the committee if you provide just what *they* want, but they may not necessarily be providing what their members

... chances are they're having a wonderful time
and thoroughly enjoying themselves and you
– they just always look like that

want. (As someone once told me, 'If our members don't take an interest in the running of the club or in voting at the A.G.M., they get the committee they deserve!') By and large, though, members and their voluntary organizers (who, remember, do have to work extremely hard) are in happy accord and the old idea that it's more important to please the committee can be ignored.

Nevertheless, always be careful how you judge your own success. Self-assessment is very difficult, but it is very important, and this applies to the standard of your performances as well. I've assumed that you have set yourself the highest musical standards, anyway, and although you do your best each time, you can always afterwards see how you could do better. And remember that the miserable-faced so-and-sos in the front row mustn't put you off – the chances are they're having a wonderful time and thoroughly enjoying themselves and you – they just always look like that. Unless of course they leave at the interval. ...

Auditions

At this stage in your career you should audition as often as you possibly can. The music press, your 'trade' press, will often carry details of auditions; we've discussed the question of radio and television auditions; orchestras and choruses through their conductors may also hold auditions. By all means let people have your cassette, but here again there is nothing to beat your physical presence, your performance, your personality, the way you put yourself across, the way that you 'sell' yourself to the audition panel or to the conductor, in conversation as well as performance.

But remember that you are never too well established, never too well known or too famous to audition, and always behave correctly at auditions. I once had to arrange an audition for a very distinguished singer with an even more distinguished conductor in a well-known concert hall. The singer went to the concert hall and went into his dressing-room and sat and waited for the conductor to come to him. Meanwhile the conductor, quite naturally, was waiting in his dressing-room for the singer to come and announce that he had arrived. The fact that the singer was on his own was partly to blame – if his agent or manager had been with him, then that person could have notified the conductor that the singer was there; but the real fault was the fact that the singer thought that he was too good, too well established, to go and knock on the door of the conductor, even though he was there because the conductor could give him work. The result was that the one never met the other.

I know that in this kind of story to give the names always adds spice, and you may well be wondering why you haven't had the actual names here, and why you haven't had the actual names in, for example, the story of the girl student who went out and treated people like dirt. Well, the reason is that I happen to know that both these people have turned over a new leaf, and there seems little point in rubbing salt in those particular ancient wounds.

The rules of deportment, dress and behaviour apply to auditions as they apply to the other areas of your career that we've already discussed.

By now you'll have gathered that at this stage of the book, although we're talking about rungs higher up the ladder, a lot of the principles are exactly the same, and I hope that they have been sufficiently drummed into you by the earlier chapters for you to see them coming. For example, the programme for your audition should be chosen just as carefully as any other, and should be designed to show you off in your best possible light. Just as when you're putting your recital programme together you should only programme music that you really feel for, music that you really understand, so in your audition you should only perform pieces that are very, very well known to you indeed and which you have proved in performance.

There is no point in thinking that a panel will be particularly impressed by one work that you have never previously performed. If, of course, they ask for a work, then that is a different matter, but if the choice is left up to you, then look at your music that you really understand, so in your audition you should only perform those, and should anything go wrong in mid performance, don't collapse completely: simply stop, and start again. An apology from the stage can embarrass an audience and an audition panel, and they are both professional enough in their own ways to know exactly what is going on and to admire you for your coolheadedness. The chances are that the round of applause at the end will be even greater.

One more pointer: this question of behaviour at auditions works two ways as well. Although you know that, no matter how famous you may be, you should never behave arrogantly towards the audition panel, or towards the conductor of the local choral society (or the audience come to that), or whomever you're auditioning for, you must be prepared from time to time to meet an arrogance, a lack of concern, a lack of consideration, from an audition panel. This may come about through nervousness, through inexperience, through shyness, or it may be a natural inbred arrogance towards the performer from someone who feels that he or she is in the driving-seat, has the whip hand, has the work to hand out, and therefore may behave badly towards you. If they do, don't rise to the bait: this is one of the things that you just have to put up with. Don't descend to their level, still behave with the utmost civility and courtesy. Remember, if you do get worked up, your performance will suffer, and they could be wanting to see how you react under stress.

Competitions

Taking part in competitions can also help in the development of your career, as long as you accept two facts before you even enter: the fact that you win doesn't necessarily mean that you have a golden career ahead of you, the fact that you do not win does not mean that that is the end of your career. A glance at gold-medal boards in music colleges will reveal some names that you have never even heard of, and if you think back to the winners of one or two competitions not so long ago, you may well wonder exactly what has happened to them. None the less some people have become internationally famous as a result of winning particular competitions.

Having been involved in the organisation of competitions and therefore in jury discussions, I've also been made very much aware of the fact that sometimes the prize has had to go to the prizewinner because of the nature of the performance but often people who may have come third or fourth have been adjudged to have greater potential, and had the prize been awarded on that basis would probably have taken home the cup based on the success that they eventually achieved in future years.

And here a little warning story: after one competition in which I'd been involved, at a private reception for the winner, an agent gatecrashed the reception and signed the winner up on the spot. The people at that time escorting the winner were delighted, and my admonitions were in vain. The reason that I had issued a warning was simply that the choice of an agent has to be a considered thing, and I knew that this particular agent was anxious to snap up the winner very much for personal publicity reasons for the agency (fair enough), and I knew that on the books there was already an artist with the same skills and of a similar standing, who was being heavily promoted by that agency. While some agencies dealing with lots of clients may have enormous lists of sopranos, altos, tenors and basses when it comes to soloists, and therefore be able to provide a marvellous service all round, this particular agency could not afford at that time to have two stars of a similar brightness, and sure enough, the winner of the particular competition who had been snatched did not shine as brightly as she might have done had she gone to a different agency as a star in her own right.

Our old friend the *British Music Yearbook* contains a very comprehensive list of competitions but – and this advice will come again in Chapter 13 – beware of regarding competitions as an extension of your student days. There's nothing worse in the profession than the perpetual student, endlessly seeking well-defined excuses for not stepping out fully into the big wide world.

Remember also that in appearing in competitions your talents will be indirectly brought to the attention of people who could well use you in other areas. For example, on the audition panel for one particular competition there may be a conductor or a festival director who will be delighted to offer you a booking in some future season. Alternatively, if you take part in the kind of competition where the semifinals or finals or both are covered by television, then clearly music-club organisers are likely to watch and could well be particularly taken by your performance and appearance.

Further Self-Promotion and the Press

When I was talking about publicity material in Chapter 4 I mentioned the personality write-up, non-music approach. As your career is developing, while you should certainly be interested in perhaps being included among the ten best-dressed men in the country or the ten most attractive women in the country or the groups most likely to succeed, you should concentrate a little on getting non-specific publicity in the music press. One advert showing all your forthcoming bookings can be very impressive (as long as it also shows how you can be contacted) and certainly you should send details of all your activities to the music press on a regular basis, but remember that copy dates differ: while an item of hot news arriving at midnight may well appear in the morning editions of the dailies, any item of diary news is more likely to be included in advance if received two or three days beforehand. Similarly for the Sunday papers, and when it comes to weekly and monthly publications the copy dates get even earlier: for the monthly music magazines for example, information should reach them at least three months beforehand. If you're sending details of your concert, then always include a photograph, for if you're very lucky they will be able to print it and this will draw specific attention to your recital as opposed to some of the others.

I have already hinted at the kind of attitude you should adopt towards your dealings with all manner of people, and this is particularly important when it comes to the press: they do like to be kept in the picture; they do like to have things to write about; they do like to have good stories to print and good concerts to review. But remember that they don't *have* to print what you send them, and that here as elsewhere, while I recommend perseverance and persistence, I *don't* recommend becoming a nuisance. And especially remember that once you've got a critic to a concert, you may not get a favourable review. If it is bad on a matter of opinion, then that is a chance you take and your attitude to a 'bad' review must reflect the help that a critic's comments can be to you. If it is inaccurate on a matter of fact, then that is a different matter. Again, this is best illustrated by a for-example story:

I gave a recital some years ago on the East Coast, and the organisers later sent me a copy of the review that appeared in the local paper. While I was not able to quarrel with the opinions that were expressed, the facts were badly wrong: in summarising the nature of the songs that I had sung the report was totally inaccurate, and gave a wrong impression of the kind of programme I had presented.

If this happens to you at the start of your career, then you will immediately realise that any potential bookers in the area reading that particular review may well be swayed by it, and you may not receive any inquiries from that area for quite some time, until the memory has died down or until somehow you have overcome it. I sought to overcome this particular incident by writing to the editor of that local paper and pointing out that the account was damaging in its inaccuracy, but to no avail, I didn't even get the courtesy of a reply. This, of course, was before the Press Council adjudication of 15 June 1978 that 'critics are entitled to be as critical as they wish to be but they should also be accurate'. Now, while certainly I could have taken it further/higher, the resultant ill-will that would have arisen would have cancelled out any benefit by having an apology printed. If you're rude to the electrician, you may never be well-lit again. I therefore let the matter drop. You're very lucky if you don't get a bad egg at one breakfast in your life. But that kind of incident thankfully is very rare, and critics and music journalists play an important role in the balancing of our musical life.

Word of Mouth Again

Similarly, word of mouth, which is so important to the development of your career, need not always be favourable. If people go along to a planning conference and say that you were fantastic and you get work, then that is marvellous for you. If however somebody goes along and says, 'Well actually I wasn't terribly impressed', then it is more than likely that you will not receive a vast amount of work as a result of that particular conference.

If on the one hand the statement is based on the fact that you gave a bad performance, or behaved badly, then that is your fault; if on the other the statement is purely an adverse personal opinion passed by a disgruntled committee member, then however unfair the comment may have been, I'm afraid you're lost – it's swings and roundabouts. If, of course, what is said is something you would wish to discuss with your legal adviser, then that again is another matter. You simply have to develop a very thick skin indeed. If you can't stand the heat, get out of the kitchen.

12
Building on the Investment
II: The Début Recital

As you'll have gathered from one of the earlier chapters in this book I personally am a great believer in début recitals. Not only do they give you a wonderful opportunity of appearing at a major hall in a fully professional concert before an audience consisting of members of the public as well as selected invitees, who will be the kind of people recommended in Chapter 5 as people in a position to give you work; but also the début recital, if properly handled and properly publicised, should bring you in at least one press cutting from a national newspaper which you will be able to quote in your brochure and which will indicate to potential bookers the professional opinion of a leading music critic as to the standard that you have achieved.

The Organisation
Having said that, I am now about to contradict the main theme of this book, which is self-help: although I have tended to promote recitals myself, whenever I have been involved in them at, say, the Wigmore Hall or the Purcell Room, either as a performer or as an organiser on behalf of young artists, even I have found latterly that it is much more sensible to have such recitals promoted by an agent. And though I'm about to give you an outline of the way in which you yourself could run a début recital, may I commend to you approaching various agents and asking them if they would be prepared to run the recital for you. The small fee that you would have to pay them for taking all the worry off your shoulders is well worth while. As you will see on reading through the list of duties to be carried out, towards the date of performance a great deal of chasing up and, therefore, possible worry is going to be involved, and frankly that is the last thing that you want to be

concerned with just before walking on to the stage in front of what could be the most important audience of your young life.

Then again, in the *British Music Yearbook* there is a list, sadly a very short list, of organisations that assist aspiring professional musicians by sponsoring recitals and promoting professional engagements. Reference has already been made to the National Federation of Music Societies, the Greater London Arts Association, and the Incorporated Society of Musicians, and in Chapter 14 I'll be saying more about the Incorporated Society of Musicians (I.S.M.) but at this stage let me put my money where my mouth is and give a credit where credit is due: Susan Alcock, the General Secretary of the I.S.M., has been present at more of my seminars than any other representative of a professional organisation and her interest and support have been much appreciated.

The Budget

If you approach an agent to manage your concert (ask around for recommendations), the chances are that they will send you a sample budget for say a Wigmore Hall or Purcell Room début recital concert. I am not giving one here, because I don't think anyone could keep up with the number of budgets, price increases and inflation changes that we're living through at this moment. So get in touch with an agent who also handles concert management or with a hall and ask them for their advice on the likely costs of a début recital. Once you have got those costs, don't be alarmed by the figures on the expenditure side: if you work extremely hard at promoting your début recital in the ways that I will explain, then there is a fairly good chance, as I have proved, that you will break even. In one case in a shared recital I even made a slight profit. (Tax man, please note: I did declare this.)

You may decide, in view of the cost, if you can't obtain any kind of sponsorship, to share the recital with friends or colleagues. Remember, if you do so, that if you split the costs in two you will also split your performing time in two, though this is not necessarily a bad thing, as was shown in the recitals which I organised with the support of Guinness and Wedgwood: each half of the début recital contained a different young artist or group and the press notices were very favourable and not skimped, even on the basis of only half a recital. Groups, of course, have another advantage: there's more of you to share the costs as well as the work.

But let's take it that you have decided to undertake the organisation of your own début recital by yourself. You will need to have some cash to hand before you even start, for example for paying the deposit for the hall, and it may be that your friendly bank manager (of whom more in Chapter 15) will be prepared to help you here.

The Date

So we're assuming that you're going ahead, against my advice, with arranging a début recital on your own with a view to getting yourself a write-up, but bearing in mind that you can never guarantee the presence of any critics whatsoever. For example, the first thing you have to do is approach the hall and book a date for your recital: you should approach them some eighteen months in advance, certainly by October for the following season, and when you book the date you should make sure as far as you can that it doesn't clash with any major musical events in the area at that time. If, for example, you're booking the Purcell Room, then check to find out what programmes or artists have been booked for the rest of the Festival Hall complex, for the Royal Albert Hall, for St John's, Smith Square, or for any other major venue that might attract the critics away from your concert. Even if you undertake this check very carefully, it could be that at the last moment there will be a sudden change of first night at Covent Garden and the critics may not be with you. It might even be a non-musical reason: a major crisis that takes over the arts page, even a newspaper strike. This is a disappointment for which you must be prepared.

If however you are casting your net extremely wide, then you will make sure that people from recording companies, festivals and concert agencies are there, and once again, as with the mailing procedure, you'll be very unlucky if out of the audience that you raise for your début recital you don't get just one booking which will cover any loss that we hope won't occur. I still remember with great gratitude the outcome of one area of my mailing in connection with a shared recital at the Purcell Room some time ago, when I wrote to all the major record companies, and out of the blue the late Cyril Stapleton came along from Pye and as a result a record of the evening was issued on the Pye label. This more than made up for the slight loss we made on that particular occasion, having given away so many complimentary tickets following so many acceptances from prospective bookers.

The Programme

Your next task will be to select the programme for your début. Apply all the rules that I've already given you on the selection of programme, and apply them with

Your début recital – get the date right

even greater stringency than before, if that is possible, because this could be a crucial programme in the early stage of your career. A great many people will recommend that you include a first performance or possibly commission a first performance, but recently critics have been advocating very strongly the inclusion of second performances. One critic suggested that a whole programme of second performances of well-received first performances would probably attract most of the major critics in London.

Publicity

Once you have selected your programme and checked with the hall to make sure that none of the items is being given just before or just after in the same hall (or for that matter that it isn't full of works that are being given in every other début recital in other halls at the time), then arrange for the printing of your programme leaflets, which will double as programme and publicity leaflet. On one side you will have, let's say, your photograph, your biography, your programme and any other relevant details; on the other side you will have the name and address of the hall, box office phone number, the date and the time of the recital, your name and what you're offering, with somewhere the kind of information that you are legally obliged to put on programmes and leaflets as passed on by the hall. The hall will advise you on the preparation of this leaflet, they will advise you on the choice of seat prices, which also have to go on the leaflet, and they will probably also be happy to advise you on the kind of printers that the majority of people who book their hall use. It's worth involving a professional designer (again friends and halls will recommend) and having lots of copies since, again, price doesn't increase too much for quantity once basic costs are covered.

With the help of the hall you will decide on the number of leaflets, and if you are having posters (which can be very useful on the Underground, for a start) then on the number of posters as well, and they will advise you on the distribution of both leaflets and posters. Here again, there are agencies that will undertake this distribution for you which have a very considerable distribution list, and quite frankly, even if you have ignored my advice on getting an agent to do the organising for you, please accept my advice on getting someone to do the distribution for you, because the bulk of the distribution happens shortly before the concert, when you will want to be practising and attending to other performance details rather than charging around, say, London, leaving leaflets in music colleges and ticket agencies and so on.

The question of press advertising will be raised by the hall, and unless you want to pay for any extra advertising, it's usual to go into the standard week-end press advertising panels showing the hall's programmes.

The Audience

Four to six weeks before the actual date of the recital (enter this instruction in your dairy), you should start sending out invitations. An agency organising the concert for you will have a complete distribution list for invitations, but if you have to devise one for yourself, then once again it can be done on the basis of the lists in the *British Music Yearbook*, which also includes a list of music critics. In writing to people, follow all the rules already given; enclose the programme leaflet about the concert, inviting the recipient of the letter to the concert and asking them to let you know if they would like complimentary (free) tickets. Again only send them tickets if they actually accept. On an occasion as important as this it is permissible and advisable to follow up your invitations with a telephone call: someone who might not have been able to make a commitment weeks in advance may well still be free on the night and not have your details to hand, so it's in your interest to jog the memory a couple of days before D (for début) Day. Short notice can be as good as long in this instance.

Remember that as well as taking care of any national publicity, for example press releases or a release on the wires of an arts news service, you should undertake a great deal of local advertising in the area where you live and in your home area if that is different. While certainly you want to invite to the début recital people who are in a position to give you write-ups or to give you work, you will also need there, for your own moral support, a good body of 'fans': family, bank manager, and supporters (as long as they don't go 'over the top' in their reaction). So don't ignore the local publicity, the domestic angle, and this is something that you will have to undertake on your own. Generally the local press will be delighted to help you, especially if the follow-up is 'Local Person Makes Good'.

The Extras

Of the other extra costs which you could accumulate if you so desired, an insurance against cancellation is probably the wisest. We'll come to the question of your own policy towards cancellation in relation to individual bookings in Chapter 14, but here I'm talking about the sad, and I hope unlikely, event of your having to cancel your début recital.

After the Guinness and Wedgwood recitals in the Purcell Room I always held a small reception for the young musicians and for those people I'd been able to persuade to come along: festival directors, journalists, agents and the like, people from the booking side of the business who could help the young artists, admittedly, but also who supported the venture because they shared my concern for the development of the careers of young musicians. I thanked them then and I thank them again now. They knew that an invitation to the party had an ulterior motive, and that was to get them to meet the young people face to face, to back up the good impression of the excellent performance with the good impression from the personality and 'social graces' of the young performer. While this would be an extra expense for you, it is a very good idea indeed. If you can't afford it, then, with the help of the hall, invite those people to come back to the green-room to meet you afterwards so at least they can have a brief chat with you. But don't run over the end of your hiring into overtime.

I hope that now you've come to the end of this particular chapter you have been thoroughly put off the idea of organising your own début recital, and will be happy to pay a management fee to an agent to do it for you, though you will still have to do a certain amount of work yourself to ensure maximum success.

Never give a début recital unless you feel you
are absolutely ready for it

13
Where the Work Comes From: Continuing

Stairway to Stardom

Quite why I chose this particular heading in my notes for the first section of this chapter I'm not sure, but it does serve to remind me that I'm assuming that we've now reached the stage where you've maintained your annual mailing for two or three years, you've built up a good series of bookings through this 'running water wears away a stone' principle and through things snowballing (the 'snowball effect' I call it), and your fees have increased to a certain extent; in fact you are now at the stage where the smaller music clubs can no longer afford you and where you are beginning to look towards some of the larger bookings, perhaps more important in view of the development of a long-term career, that you see as being necessary to making a firm and permanent career, and which up till now have eluded you in quantity.

Certainly you won't want to ignore any other bookings that may come your way, but certainly also you are now determined to set yourself on perhaps a 'higher' level as far as fees and the nature of your work is concerned. You will want, for example, to be aiming at the major national festivals rather than the local ones; you will, it may be hoped, be going for those music clubs or those schools which book major artists rather than younger artists of the type that you perhaps are now ceasing to be; you will want to aim at network radio and tv programmes in addition to local work – and all this means that from now on your mailing will be more selective, more specialised. You may even want to repeat your début recital on a self-promotion basis.

From the experience and knowledge that you've gained over the past, say, two or three years of building up your career, you'll know which particular festivals, which particular clubs, which particular schools and so on you want to aim for, so draw them out of the general mailing lists, create a special letter merely for 'the big date' and from now on make your mailings specifically to those revised lists. Here again, letters of personal recommendation from well-known performers will help. You will also by now, if you have not got an agent, be hoping that by getting these major bookings you'll be making yourself much more attractive to a larger agency, which will then take from you the need to do the full regular mailing (their list mailings will make sure your name still goes to those folk you've dropped from your own lists) but certainly not the need to follow the advice in the second part of this book.

Always remember, though, that the smaller clubs and amateur choirs or orchestras are the backbone of our musical life and mustn't be forgotten. A club that booked you often at the start of your career is one of the few cases for a return for free when famous if you can now help them. They have been the foundation of your career.

You will also have found that a pattern has emerged in your work, to put it at its simplest you'll find that you're performing for music clubs and schools, say, in the autumn, winter and early spring months, and then when those clubs shut down with the summer evenings coming along, you'll find that the festivals seem to take over, with radio, TV and general work spread fairly evenly throughout the year. As this pattern is emerging you may have slight kittens at a certain lack of bookings along the way, but very soon you'll gain the confidence of knowing that this is the way that the gaps in your engagement diary will fill up.

The Fall-back

But it may be that you haven't in fact enjoyed the kind of success that I described in the previous paragraph; you may feel that the time has come for you to be a little more basic in your back-up work while you continue to persevere with the lists suggested in Chapter 5.

Although again these are suggestions that will take you perhaps sliding back towards being a perpetual student, it is important that I include them in this chapter so that you are aware of some of the other resources apart from secretarial work or charring that can help you to have a basic income either in your very first one or two years of attempting this kind of mailing exercise, or later on if you have not yet achieved the success that you feel you deserve and will ultimately come your way.

Grants, Awards and Scholarships

Assuming that you have decided that you must have some kind of financial assistance at this early stage in your career or that you feel, having left college, that you do need a little more study before you are ready to launch yourself into the competitive world of music, then again without (please) becoming a perpetual student, you should refer to the *British Music Yearbook*, where there is a very helpful section on scholarships, grants and awards, several of which should be suitable for you to try for help in overcoming the problem that is facing you.

Teaching

I'm certainly not referring to teaching as a fall-back in relation to performing. I can well remember those applicants for places at the Guildhall School of Music and Drama who when asked what they would do if they didn't obtain a place on the Performers' Course, replied that they would try for the Teachers' Course. Teaching is a very, very important career indeed and should only be undertaken if it is something that you really want to do. If you are only thinking of teaching as a way of earning a little bit of extra money and your heart is not really in it, then for your sake and the sake of those that you will be instructing, please keep well away.

The fact remains, however, that many people do add to their income in early years by undertaking a certain amount of teaching. It could be that you will advertise to give private teaching locally, it could be that you will make yourself available to your local music adviser for a certain amount of teaching in schools, or again you could obtain a temporary position in a school or music college.

Chorus and Orchestral Work

Here again I would not wish to imply that this sort of work is a fall-back for someone who is not quite making the grade in a solo career, although again there are a number of distinguished soloists who in their early days developed their career while singing or playing in one or other of the excellent choruses and orchestras that exist in the professional music world.

To audition you should get in touch for a chorus with the chorus secretary, for an orchestra with the orchestral manager; if it is an opera chorus or orchestra in which you wish to appear to supplement your income, then you should approach the general administrator of the opera company of your choice. But do beware of undertaking any kind of regular commitment that might interfere with the work that you are being offered as a soloist if it is only a soloist that you want to be. I will look at this more closely in the next chapter when we consider the problems of cancellation. There are, of course, many professional musicians who prefer to combine a solo career with, for example, an orchestral career and do it most happily and successfully.

Keyboard
Clearly here I'm talking specifically to keyboard players who are finding it difficult to make their way in a solo career. Offer yourself as an accompanist: accompaniment is by no means a second-string activity, accompanists being just as important as the people they accompany (and as a duo you can follow all the advice in the first part of the book and share the effort as well as the cost); and as I'm sure you will know, if you are a keyboard player, there are opportunities for *répétiteur* work with opera companies of varying sizes, and of course you'll be familiar with working for ballet classes, choral societies and the like. But this is a useful reminder of one other way of supplementing your income.

But Only Temporary
A reminder that if you do go in for a grant, award or scholarship, or some supplementary teaching, chorus or keyboard work, and it is only to supplement your income while you are trying to make the grade as a soloist on the recital or the concert platform, do not fall into the trap of taking things easy and giving up the push. If, of course, you find that the award or grant or scholarship leads you into an area of study that you wish to pursue or that teaching becomes a vocation or that your chorus work leads to solo opera performance or your *répétiteur* work to conducting, then naturally I wish you well. If however it is only a temporary expedient, remember to treat it as such and make this clear to the people who are employing you so that they are not disillusioned when you suddenly up and off.

The Icing on the Cake
Once you have established your basic pattern of work and are trying to find your way into bigger festivals and major concerts, you can supplement your income very enjoyably by entering into what could perhaps be the lighter side of the world of music. There is always scope for employment in summer shows (which could take up a lot of your time) and in musicals, and here you will find that bookings are usually handled by agents with either a lighter side to their agency or who specialise in this kind of work; then there are cruises, for which you should get in touch with

the entertainment officers of cruise lines, and holiday camps even: on one charity, student-days tour in Lincolnshire, Butlins at Skegness, to help our finances, gave us free meals and accommodation in return for some entertainment. With me as compère the correct mass-audience response to my cry of, 'Are you happy *then*?' was 'O.K. *Len*!'

If you have a particular affinity for lighter music, then it may be that you will wish to make your career permanently in this area after a brief sampling. It certainly is worth trying and I have always felt that a broadly based repertoire and broadly based experience can only be good even for someone who regards him or herself as primarily a 'serious' performer. Then again, someone has to write and record or play the music for stage plays (provincial rep and the National Theatre and Royal Shakespeare Company, for example), for films, for commercials, a difficult world to break into but another source of icing for what I hope by now is developing for you into a very tasty cake.

Session Work

Mention of commercials and films leads us on to session work. If after two or three years you have become well known in the musical world and if you have maintained contact with previous colleagues who are now working in choruses or orchestras, and if you are an extremely good sight-reader, then you may find yourself being called upon by those people responsible for booking *ad hoc* groups for working in recording studios, for providing music for films or commercials, for backing groups, for Muzak-type tapes and so on.

There is work here available for both singers and players, and of course you may also get *ad hoc* work in choruses and orchestras. If you have built up a reputation for being efficient and reliable as well as a good all-round musician, then people will be very keen to offer you this kind of work. The trouble is, as I have been told many times, that it usually comes your way when you are a well-established musician and perhaps don't have as much time for it as you would like to, rather than when you are at the start of your career and really need the kind of contacts and opportunities and finance that session work will bring to you.

14
Setting Your Affairs in Order:
The Advice

Having I hope got your career sorted out, I must now, before the closing chapters, turn my attention to getting the rest of your life in order. These matters need attention from the very word go while you're assembling the material you're going to send out to get work.

Private Life
When I first typed out one of the earlier chapters in this book, I intended to type the words, 'This is to help you to live and exist'. Instead I typed the words, 'help you to *love* and exist'. (Almost as good as 'get in tough with an agent'.)

But this was a good reminder to me that before I get into the technical side of setting your affairs in order, I must make mention of the fact that a career in this world of music can have a disruptive effect on your private life. If at one or two previous stages in this book you have felt that I was sounding like an agony columnist, well this is where I will sound like one even more, and I don't mind doing so: I've always had the kind of face that people brought their troubles to, I'm always the person who gets asked for directions in the street ('No, I'm afraid I can't tell you how to get to the Memorial Hall').

If you're a loner, if you live on your own, then you'll have no problems in keeping the kind of unearthly hours one has to in this career or spending a great deal of time addressing envelopes or touring or practising (taking the neighbours into consideration, of course). But do remember that this sort of freelance life, particularly when it comes to close contact with colleagues or bookers, permanently or temporarily, can have a disruptive effect on any kind of relationship, particularly on a marriage, and on a marriage where there are children. If your partner is also a performing musician, then you may have a greater degree of understanding or conversely a greater amount of problems. (They say that when a booker rings up the work is never for the partner that answers the phone.)

But do make absolutely sure, before you embark on a career in music, that both you and those you live with are aware of the problems that might arise. Enough said.

Professional Organisations

It's very important that you should join one or more of the three major professional organisations in the musical world.

The M.U. (Musicians' Union) caters for orchestral players, and it's impossible to be a professional orchestral player in Great Britain without joining it.

Equity (The British Actors Equity Association) is for theatrical performers and producers, and this means singers in opera, both solo and chorus singers, in musicals and the like, as well as straight actors and actresses.

Both the M.U. and Equity are trade unions in the full sense.

The I.S.M. (Incorporated Society of Musicians) whose members are almost exclusively those who regard themselves as soloists (vocal and instrumental), conductors, teachers or a combination of these, isn't a trade union though it is concerned about rates of remuneration as well as other things.

The addresses of all these organisations, from whom you can get full details of all they can offer you, are to be found at the back of this book, and they have all drawn up standard contracts for their members.

Contracts and Agreements

The use of the kind of contract form available from the professional organisations mentioned in the previous section will keep you clear of a great many of the kind of difficulties that can arise as the result of misunderstandings or inadequate confirmation of arrangements. But if you don't use one of these forms, then if you stick to the kind of basic office system that I recommended earlier in the book, and confirm all the necessary details in writing, and have them confirmed by the booker in writing as well, you shouldn't go far wrong.

If you do undertake any *ad hoc* session work then you may find that this is merely confirmed by telephone, and this kind of gentleman's agreement in the music profession is really just as binding and must be just as closely observed.

Cancellation

We've had various trailers for this paragraph throughout the book, and it can be one of the nightmare situations met by the young musician without an agent. If a booking has been confirmed by an agent and any kind of cancellation is necessary, let's say at this stage through illness, then that agent will be able to find a replacement for the client.

If however a booking is made direct with you, then you should always have one or two people up your sleeve who offer virtually the same kind of professional performance services as you do, so that, if you are taken ill at the last minute, you are in a position to offer the client a replacement yourself.

Obviously you should try to keep as healthy as possible, as I've already said, but illness and accident can strike very suddenly, and with the best will in the world you may find yourself unable to fulfil an engagement.

But also from time to time you may find that having accepted one engagement, perhaps a one-off engagement for a small music club, you are offered, let's exaggerate for the sake of this example, a tour in America. What you don't do is simply accept the tour in America and completely forget about the one-off engagement. The correct thing to do is immediately approach the person who has offered you the one-off engagement, explain apologetically that you've been offered a tour in America and what a tremendous opportunity it is for you, and would he be kind enough to release you from the single engagement. You have a replacement to offer him, and if his club is going to be involved in any extra expenses like re-advertising, you could offer to contribute. You will find that bookers in the music business, if approached in the correct and honest and straightforward manner, will be most cooperative.

Every now and then however you will find yourself in an unfortunate, perhaps short-notice cancellation, situation through no fault of your own, and just as in some instances you have to have a very thick skin, and swallow your pride, and take the rough with the smooth, and any other cliché available, then when this happens – well, let me give you a for-example. ...

I mentioned in the section on Annual Mailings a booking that I was given as a result of persevering. This was in fact with a theatre, which I'd always wanted to visit with my one-man show. The booking had been confirmed, when I was contacted by an organisation that uses me regularly in the presentation area of my life, in connection with a whole series of presentations in which I was the key part, and for which I'd been given the dates some time beforehand. It became very

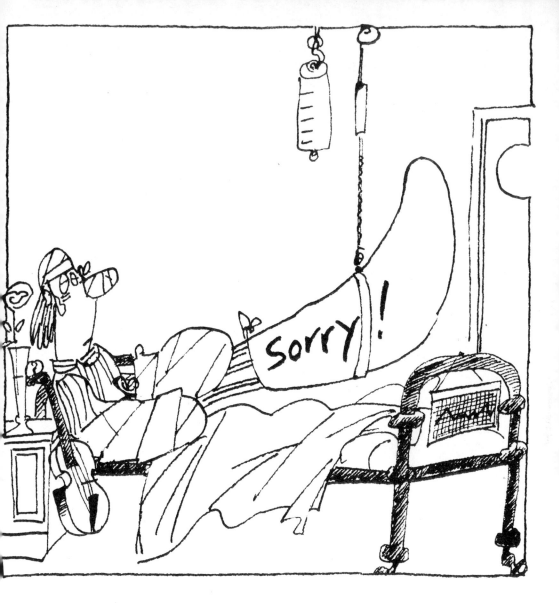

With the best will in the world
you may find yourself unable to fulfil an engagement

quickly clear in the course of conversation that the dates that had been confirmed to me were wrong, and one of the dates as part of this complete series was the date for which I had been confirmed with the theatre.

Because of this error there hadn't been any question of first-come first-served or pencilling versus confirmation, but it was obvious that while my own up-the-sleeve musical replacement could go to the theatre if the organisers agreed, the series of presentations of which I was the key part could not possibly go ahead without me. I was therefore put in the embarrassing position, the booking having been made direct, of contacting the theatre and saying that I would not after all be able to carry out the booking. Quite justifiably, although the error was no fault of mine, they were upset, and this is the kind of sad memory that one does have to cope with from time to time.

(N.B. This is the last of the few personal 'for-examples' in this book, but as they've nearly all been on problems (well, a catalogue of triumphs would bring joy to my heart but bore the pants off you) please re-read the sleeve at this point to remind yourself how marvellous I am and to correct any impression you might have formed that the life of the person offering you advice has consisted only of disasters.)

The warning just now, 'beware the regular commitment' if you want to build up a solo career in the recital or concert field is particularly relevant in this 'cancellation' section. If you have undertaken a job that involves you every Wednesday evening, or if you have undertaken any kind of commitment that involves you being in a regular place at a regular time, you will find it very difficult to balance out this kind of permanent long-term agreement, albeit only on a part-time basis, with the haphazard arrival of dates that can fall on any day of the week and in any week; and you may find yourself having to turn down some of the very one-off bookings that you've gone to so much trouble to get. So, if you do have any kind of regular commitment, make sure that you have the option to put in a deputy or to cancel at short notice if necessary, otherwise a lot of your effort in building up solo engagements will be completely wasted if you have to refuse them because of a regular commitment that is only intended to be a fall-back and a basic financial security.

The final thought on cancellation has to be that from time to time the cancellation will come from the booker, from the client. Very often, if a client has to cancel out on a date you will be offered another date instead, and clearly this is the most satisfactory way out. But sometimes it will be a straight cancellation and here, if you don't have the backing of an agent or a professional organisation or a contract, you will have to cope with the situation on your own.

Usually the best solution is to agree some kind of cancellation fee depending on how close to the actual date the cancellation has been notified. Fifty per cent of the agreed fee is a good cancellation fee for a cancellation notified reasonably in advance, but if it is a last-minute cancellation and thus there is little chance of your finding other work, or possibly if you have turned down other work that can't be retrieved for the date in question, then you should hold out for the full amount. This is where some of the advisers covered in the next chapter will come in handy.

Fees and Expenses

This is yet another area that I have been setting you up for with various mentions as you have worked your way through this musician's survival kit. The question of fees is one of the most difficult on which to offer advice, and this is really an area about which you should talk as much as possible with your friends and colleagues to work out your own policy. Your first decision clearly is where to start on the fee scale, and wherever you start I beseech you not to start too low. Although clubs appreciate low fees, too low and they think you can't be any good.

The B.B.C. have a very efficient and very well organised booking service, and for certain programmes and activities they do have set rates, but as budgets are limited, clearly when you first have contact with them the fee that you will be offered will not be particularly high, except in special circumstances. Once you have accepted that fee, it will be on your card for some time, and you may find it difficult to raise.

The same thing applies to the fee that you put on your brochure first of all. If you find it inadequate in your first year, too high a jump will make people think twice before booking you, even though, had you started at that higher-jump fee in the first place, things might have been different. (Though paradoxically when you're doing really well and you put your fee up dramatically so as to cut down the number of bookings offered, you may well find yourself in ever-greater demand.) It is not difficult to get hold of agency lists (colleges and bookers should have them) and see at what level people you regard as being your equals are charging. Similarly, if you look at an artist that you admire and see what kind of fee you have to work for, this will enable you to establish your basic fee. Here you will find the advice of one of the professional organisations invaluable, because although fees are often laid down for chorus members, for session singers, for orchestral players and the like, it is very difficult to lay down a definite fee for a solo artist on the recital or concert platform.

The problem of expenses can be just as difficult if you don't have a set policy. My advice always is to quote a fee, plus expenses (except possibly in your immediate base area) plus where applicable VAT (more on that shortly) and if it includes your accompanist. If an organiser knows that your basic fee is the same wherever you are in the country, and that on top of that you will charge travelling expenses and overnight accommodation if necessary, then that organiser will know exactly where he or she stands. If conversely you have a fee that is inclusive of expenses, then make absolutely sure that those included expenses will be high enough to cover, say, a visit to the north of Scotland. It is because this kind of inclusion will exaggerate the fee so much that I prefer the system of quoting a basic fee plus expenses.

I've already talked about the question of fee negotiation. You must work out also your own policy to charity requests: if you are offered expenses only, then make absolutely sure that everybody understands you are going for expenses, and that that sum is not your fee. You will find as you climb the ladder of success that you will be asked more and more often to give up your time for charity. No matter how warm-hearted you may be, remember that you are freelance and that you are out to earn a living, to pay the rent and rates, to keep the wife and child in the manner to which they have become accustomed.

Many artists only perform for certain charities and politely but regretfully turn down approaches from other charities. There are charities which prefer to pay your full fee, but if it is a question of half-fee or expenses only, then the negotiation logic comes into play and I would recommend you say full fee or nothing. If you do accept to go for free it is a good idea to make it clear to the charity that you accept on a 'professional engagements permitting' basis, that is, if you do get offered a paid job on the same day, then the charity will understand that you have to earn a living and will release you. Even with charities, the half-fee 'devaluation of currency' syndrome can apply: sometimes they don't seem to realise that you are effectively making a donation of half your fee to the charity – charging the full amount then handing back a cheque for half the sum would make it clearer. But don't be upset if early on you have to turn down charity requests: the time will come. And in these early days charity definitely begins at home.

15
Setting Your Affairs in Order: The Advisers

Agents and Managers

Another reminder; the reason that you have been undertaking the kind of exercise recommended in the first part of this book is either because you haven't got an agent who manages you exclusively, or because you are on the books of a number of agents none of whom will promote you exclusively and therefore you have to undertake that kind of exercise yourself; or because you have no agent at all.

Another assumption has to be that you are working towards the stage where you would like to have an exclusive agent. If you do get offered this kind of sole representation contract by an agent, remember that all your bookings will go through that agency (even those still arising out of your own efforts), and the agency will be responsible for getting you work. The kind of advice that is given in this book refers to management as well as agency in relation to your own career. If you have been following my advice, you have been acting as your own manager as well as your own agent, and my definition of a manager is somebody who will look after your career, who will go out of his or her way to develop it, and who will offer you the kind of advice that I am offering you now as to contacts, behaviour and the kind of bookings at which you should be aiming yourself.

So only take on an exclusive agency agreement if you feel that proper management will be involved, that you'll get enough to live on and that the agency wasn't just after a part of the action and won't simply sit back and take commission on all the work that comes in thanks to your efforts in the past and will do nothing about developing your career in the future. Sometimes, in spite of a lot of pushing, an agency just can't help an artist or the relationship just doesn't click. If this happens, part on good terms, it's really nobody's fault, and find someone with whom you do click and who can get you work. Often when you move from smaller to larger bookings you may feel you need to move from a smaller to a larger or better-known agency: this can be disheartening for the agent who hopefully nurtured your young talent, but if you really must move, then it's you you have to think of. But never forget the part that that agent's work played in your career.

If, of course, you are lucky and do extremely well, then you will be able to employ a manager to handle your affairs for you, to deal with agents and bookers, to cope with your annual mailings, your hotel and travel arrangements, and keep his ear to the ground in the way that agents do, so that you will know what kind of B.B.C. programmes are in the pipeline, what kind of themes are being planned for festivals – so that you are in there with a chance with everybody else.

Secretaries

The logical development in this area, having set up your own office system and either managed it yourself or shared a secretary with others, is to have your own secretary. If you are able to afford to have your own manager and your own secretary, then you *are* doing extremely well, and I congratulate you, and hope that you will now rush out and buy a large number of copies of this book to which you owe all your success, and present them free of charge to students about to emerge from music colleges so that they may enjoy in due course the advantages that you are enjoying now.

Your Finances

The professional organisation(s) to which you belong will be very happy to advise you on such problems as income tax and value-added tax (VAT), but here I come to another extreme, the other end of the line that began with advising you to do all this kind of mailing exercise on your own because the chances are you won't have an agent to do it for you, then moved through the situation whereby I advised you to employ an agent to manage your début recital but at the same time gave you advice on how to do it yourself, right through to this present situation where although I could devote a great deal of time to how to manage income tax, the kind of allowances you can claim and what to do about VAT, I fear that my advice will be simply, 'Get yourself a good accountant.'

An Accountant – Income Tax and VAT

Ask round among your friends and colleagues and the professionals you meet, to find out who they use, what they are charged and if they are satisfied. In a way this should be your very first task, because if it isn't, then I will have to advise you on what to do between now, reading this book, and the time you actually get yourself an accountant, and I don't want to do that because I want you to get an accountant as soon as you possible can.

Your accountant, who should definitely know about our world of music, will tell you immediately exactly how to look after your finances, how to run a bank book and a cash book, how to check your bank statements, how to keep all the receipts that you get for those expenses which he will advise you as being allowable against tax. The reason I'm so dogmatic in this particular piece of advice is that when I first went freelance, with an economics degree including statistics tucked under my belt and business accountancy experience, I handled all my own financial affairs and dealt with the tax man myself. The relationship was a very amiable one, but when the amount of work got too much and I found myself an accountant, I discovered just how stupid I'd been trying to handle it on my own.

Your accountant will also be able to guide you on the fee question if your answer to that problem hasn't yet appeared, perhaps by suggesting that you decide how much you want to earn next year, the number of jobs you want to take on, and divide one into the other to get a guideline. He will also be able to convince you as to the monetary value to put on your own time: so that if buying self-sealing envelopes seems more expensive than licking ordinary ones you'll see how your time thus spent is worth more than the extra envelope cost; similarly employing an agent to run your début will release a great deal of your time that can be put to other financial use and bring in more in the long run than the agent's management fee.

In the *British Music Yearbook* there are extremely useful articles on income tax and VAT, and if you read these straight away I think they will convince you even more of the sense of having a good accountant, and leaving the advice needed on both these areas very much in his hands and making his fee also money well spent. I am one of the people who advocate that you should be registered for VAT even before you achieve the income level at which registration is compulsory. If you are not registered for VAT you will find yourself in the position of not being able to charge VAT on your services while at the same time having to pay the VAT charged by other people. In my opinion the extra effort needed to cope with a separate VAT column in your bank book and your cash book is well worth the extra financial return to you.

Insurance Generally

One of the easiest ways of making sure that you are properly insured, and that you are reminded regularly as to when those various insurance policies fall for renewal, so that you don't in a busy life forget to renew them and suddenly find that you are not covered, is to get yourself an insurance broker. Once again, ask round among your friends for someone who understands the particular needs of the self-employed musician. He will be able to advise you on the best way to insure your home, its contents, your personal belongings as you travel around, your car, and your life. You can obtain advice on all these areas from your professional organisation, and they do operate various special schemes, but here as in the other areas in this chapter, I would advocate a combination of your own expert and your professional organisation. You don't pay an insurance broker as you pay an accountant – he gets commission from the companies he deals with.

As a self-employed person you must think also of some kind of pension scheme for your old age (the earlier you start the better), some kind of instrument insurance if you play an instrument, and some kind of health and sickness insurance. This should cover, first, the sort of scheme whereby if you suddenly have an illness that requires you to go into hospital and you can't afford private treatment, you don't have to wait for ages and lose work until a National Health bed is available. By joining such a scheme operated, say, by the Bristol Contributary Welfare Association or BUPA or Private Patients Plan, then for a certain sum each year, you are covered so that the moment that you are ill you will be able to go straight into hospital and have all the costs fully taken care of as well as yourself. Many professional organisations do in fact operate group-discount schemes with companies like B.C.W.A., P.P.P. and BUPA, so contact your professional organisation about this.

You should also take out some kind of insurance so that if you are temporarily disabled so can't work but do not have to go into hospital, and are therefore not covered by the kind of scheme just mentioned, then you do receive a basic amount of money each week that helps you to meet the kind of expenses that have to be met before you start living, such as rent, rates or mortgage repayments. Insurance against loss of specific fees or fees generally can be expensive.

National Insurance

This is an area in which your accountant and professional organisation will be able to give you advice and, of course, you can call at your local office of the

Department of Health and Social Security. Although National Insurance will be a regular outgoing for you, you won't necessarily have to go every week to the Post Office to buy your stamp. It is possible to buy it on the basis of a standing order through your bank (this is good because it means you don't miss payments and so avoid the risk of losing benefits) or again you may apply with the help of your accountant for deferment of payments, and, if granted, you will be charged the appropriate amount at the end of the year in question when you pay your income tax for it.

Savings

Because of this and because of other outgoings for which you must budget, I recommend that you start some kind of savings scheme immediately. Self-employed people can be notoriously spendthrift, and the moment the money goes in and there seems to be a reasonable balance, the money is liable to go out again. But do remember that at the end of the year you will have income tax to pay; you will also have National Insurance to pay; then there are your annual insurance premiums and subscriptions and so on. The easiest and most painless way of providing for these and the rainy day and the little extras is saving by the kind of drip-feed arrangement whereby each month a regular amount goes either into a deposit account or into a building-society account or into some other kind of savings account, so quietly you hardly notice or miss it. But it builds up. Your bank manager (see below) will advise you here and later on investments.

Security

While on insurance, there are some points arising from previous areas in the book. When, for example, you leave a message on your answering-machine, don't leave the kind that will let any burglar who happens to phone know exactly how long you are out. And it is very tempting to get publicity about your overseas tours in the press, but if your address is well known locally, then what happened to some friends of mine could happen to you: they were a husband and wife who were away at the same time for different reasons and the local press ran an article saying what a marvellous coincidence this was and how exciting for them both. It wasn't particularly exciting when they got home and found their house completely ransacked. Save the publicity for when you get back.

It is for this kind of reason that radio and television programmes don't usually give an address when they are wishing somebody a happy holiday or playing a record for someone on holiday: it is tantamount to announcing to all the burglars in the area that this property is vacant for a certain period of time. So do get the advice of your local Crime Prevention Officer so that your residence is fully secured. If you do this, and you are also well insured, preferably with an index-linked replacement value, then should the worst come to the worst you will be well covered and not have the awful agony of having to find money to replace stolen goods as well as money on which to live.

And just on this subject of going away on tour, echoing back to the question of income tax, it doesn't really do to try to keep things from your income tax inspector. If by any chance you're thinking of holding back the cash payments that were made to you when you went on tour in a particular area (cash-payment temptations are better avoided), or if the local press have made great play of that tour or the fact that you have just come back from a series of very successful concerts on the Continent, and your tax man reads the local press and then sees your return without those particular figures on it, well, need I say more?

Doctor and Solicitor

The name and phone number of your accountant and your insurance broker should appear in your diary, together with the name of your doctor and his or her phone number and also the name and phone number of your solicitor.

I'm not suggesting for a moment that you're about to indulge in illegal activities, but in one or two instances in the book I have referred to situations where you may require legal advice, and it is best to be prepared for the unexpected. In any event you have to make a will.

Bank Manager

Last but not least, as they say. Your bank manager could well be the most important person to you at the outset of your career. Not only will he be able to help you keep your financial affairs directly in order by maintaining constant touch with you and with your accountant (they will both help you budget), but he may also be able to assist you in a practical way.

If for example you have costed out the kind of mailing exercise advised in the first part of this book and you find that you do not have the capital available to undertake it immediately, then go and see your bank manager and discuss it with him. If he is suitably impressed that you have the talent, and that you have the will power, and that you intend to set about the exercise in the proper manner, then he

... go and see your bank manager

may well be prepared to allow you an overdraft or a small loan to meet the cost of the exercise. He may suggest that you don't undertake quite such an exhaustive mailing as I have recommended, and because this is now towards the end of the book, I can give you a let-out here and say that it is possible to undertake only a partial mailing if you do feel that you haven't really got the time and money for a full one.

It may be that in the first place you will only mail music clubs and festivals (a total of some 600), then on the basis of the resulting bookings get in touch with music advisers and radio and television on the 'build-up clump' or '*en route*' basis (Chapter 10). In any event, if you do only undertake a selective mailing, then as far as the other headings are concerned, you should conduct a blitz in your own home area. Also try pointing out to your bank manager that by undertaking this work yourself, because you haven't got an agent, there isn't going to be a percentage taken off any particular fee and the percentages that you are saving could, as it were, go towards the cost of the overdraft or the bank loan.

Your bank manager or your accountant should also be able to advise you, should you require the help of a mortgage broker (and the sooner you get property round you the better) or any other kind of official or financial help during the course of your career. Your professional organisation(s), which by now you will see why it is essential for you to join, will be able to offer you similar practical advice.

Envoi

All the advisers that I have referred to in this chapter are very important to you. You should expand your filing system with a section for each, and you should keep them in the picture as to the development of your career. If you are giving a concert or a recital in their area of work or home, then invite them, and in this instance send them tickets first of all. They might be even more impressed if you ask them to pay! If they can come along, and see that you are making a go of your career, and that you are making an effort to develop it, then they will be that much more closely behind you and will give you that much more support.

It could well be a very good move indeed to show them this book, so that they will know exactly the kind of serious effort you are making to get your career and your private affairs in good order. It would also help if you show this book to the people who book you. It will help them to understand your problems and realise that you are thinking of theirs. Once again, it is two-way traffic, and you will have the best of both worlds.

16
Over to You

Yes, that does sound rather like the title of a twenties musical, or perhaps a rather bad colloquial translation of the title of a Mozart opera, but in either event, it's now very much over to you. Even though you'll have this book to help you, at this stage of your career you're definitely on your own.

The first time that you read these words will be as you end your complete read-through of the book. The second time will be following your second read-through when you've actually carried out the advice that I've given you. The most important thing at this stage, first time round, will be your attitude of mind. Some people have said to students planning to take this advice, 'If you're any good, then you don't need to do that sort of thing'. That again is one of those statements that by and large simply isn't true.

There may be one or two professionals at the very top of their tree who've led a charmed life, who've had an exclusive agent from the moment they left music college, and have never had to worry about anything other than performing; but if you ask around you'll find that almost every other musician has endeavoured to undertake this kind of exercise in one form or another without having had the advantage of it all being set down as comprehensively as it now is.

Accept that this is an advantage, that if you do follow my advice you'll be streets ahead of those of your 'competitors' who don't. What happens if everybody does it? Experience has shown that everybody won't, that some of the students who enthusiastically take down notes at the seminars baulk at the idea of the amount of work, and I've no doubt that a number of you reading this book will also feel that you just can't take it on.

Please try to overcome your shyness or distaste, try to overcome the feeling that you simply can't cope, because, as with everything, once you've started it's amazing how quickly you actually achieve your ends. And if everybody did do it, well, echoing what I've said several times throughout the book, it would be marvellous for 'both sides'. Remember that in the arts, supply creates demand.

Perseverance is now required, perseverance and confidence. Under-confidence can be just as damaging to this sort of exercise as it can be to your performance on stage.

There are still other areas to which you can turn your attention, overseas for example, and here you can obtain advice from the British Council. But for now I think I've given you quite enough to think about.

The success won't happen overnight, but once you've undertaken the mailing, and once you've set your affairs in order, and once you've carried out all the advice to help yourself and to help those who book you, you'll find that the snowball effect will start and that the discipline this kind of organisation demands will benefit you in other areas.

This book was written to help solve a problem and, thank goodness, other people are becoming aware of the difficulties of young musicians at the start of their career. Although the Gulbenkian Report on Training Musicians only gives it a brief mention towards the end, at least it's there and at least the evidence was taken; there have been television programmes and radio programmes in which I've found myself involved; there have been articles in the press.

So do raise this issue at every possible opportunity: the more people become aware of it, the more people see this book, the more people that meet you and talk to you and know what you're having to do to launch yourself into the world of music, then the more chance there is that in the next edition I'll be able to report more new ideas and developments to the advantage of all young musicians.

Some Useful Addresses

Not a long list, as once you have your copy of the *British Music Yearbook* you'll have all the addresses you need there. These are those of the main organisations on a national basis mentioned in the text. Local references or mentions on a passing basis (a regional arts association, local radio station, or concert hall for example) will be found in the complete lists for that category in the *BMYb*.

British Actors' Equity Association, 8 Harley Street, London W1N 2AB
01 636 6367

Incorporated Society of Musicians, 10 Stratford Place, London W1N 9AE
01 629 4413

Mechanical-Copyright Protection Society Ltd, 380 Streatham High Road, London SW16 6HR   01 769 3181

Musicians' Union, 29 Catherine Place, Buckingham Gate, London SW1E 6EH
01 834 1348

National Federation of Music Societies, 1 Montague Street, London WC1B 5BS
01 580 4885

Postscript
GOOD LUCK